All the best

"Scott has written an important book on one of the most important issues facing the biopharma industry: the trust that has been eroded from the customers of the industry. Scott helps to frame what has happened in the last 20 years that has led to loss of access, an inability to partner with key customers, and the value proposition of the industry called into question.

This is an important book on many levels as Scott helps the reader to see the interconnected elements of events that have forced an industry to cut its field force by half and recreate its commercial model. The book goes on to suggest practical solutions grounded in trusting behaviors and a set of initiatives the industry can take to rebuild trust with its customers.

This is a must read for strategists and those accountable for implementation in the biopharma field. I would suggest Marketing, Medical Affairs, Account Management, and Sales take the time to read this book to help them at a time when the science has never been more exciting and the access more restricted."

John Harrington

Former Chief Commercial Officer - Sanofi Oncology

"From supervising US airmen at a nuclear missile facility to personally manning the front lines of the healthcare revolution, Scott Costin views the business of biopharma sales through a unique prism. In 1999, with a former US Air Force officers' can-do attitude, Scott began a career in biopharma sales in the Pacific Northwest—often considered one of the most inhospitable regions to manufacturers of newly approved drugs and medical devices. This early work gave him visibility to changing views on relationships between healthcare providers and healthcare suppliers. He came through successfully to the other side and is a valued partner for providers and executives at Academic Medical Centers and Integrated Delivery Networks.

Scott is a true health care leader. In his book, *The Doctor Won't See You Now*, the reader gets a front row seat for a lesson on how we got to where we are today. If you are employed in biopharma sales, this book is a must read. This is a rope to help you escape the rut you may currently be occupying. If you are considering a career in biopharma sales, buy this book. And, if when you are done reading it, you still think you have what it takes, come join the ranks of this fulfilling career."

Jeff Kline

Vice President, Sales, Allergan – PLC

"Limited physician access is increasingly common for pharmaceutical representatives and can be particularly daunting for a new sales representative. This book provides a perspective regarding contributors to the problem, and most importantly provides practical solutions and approaches to address the challenge. If you are new to the pharmaceutical industry and looking for ways to overcome access challenges in your territory, this book provides good ideas."

Doug Randall

EVP of Commercial and Business Operations, Tenax Therapeutics

---

"As a former sales representative, sales manager, and brand marketing lead, I found this book to hit just the right points from both a historical as well as forward-looking perspective. Scott offers great advice in an easy to read fashion that should be executed urgently in order to restore trust in the biopharma representative/healthcare customer relationship. While the role of the biopharma representative will continue to evolve, it remains an important channel to provide those making critical treatment decisions with appropriate information and resources. Done right, a representative can and should be a valuable part of the health eco-system. This is a great "how-to" for any representative looking to succeed in the healthcare system, matching the right treatments with the right patients and keeping people healthier longer!"

Angela Moskow

Interim Head, North American Government Relations, Sanofi

"The dynamics and complexity of the US healthcare system are constantly changing. This book provides a clear and concise summary of how many of these changes have impacted the healthcare prescriber, which in turn has dramatically impacted the role and life of the biopharma sales representative. It is a great resource with easy to understand and fundamental steps necessary to be a successful biopharma sales representative today. I would encourage anyone considering a role in biopharma sales and even those already in the industry to read this book."

John Timberlake

CEO, Valeritas Holdings, Inc.

"Scott has done quite a service for those who aspire to a career in biopharma sales/sales leadership. Drawing from nearly 20 years of experience across a broad range of responsibilities, Scott provides an unvarnished look at the challenges, roadblocks, risks, and rewards of a career in biopharma and, most importantly, the coaching and examples needed to be successful."

Kevin Madden

US Sales Manager, InHealth Technologies

"As a veteran of the rapidly changing pharmaceutical sales world, Scott brings a real world perspective to the challenges facing the pharma sales executive. Whether one is new to the industry or has years of experience, the recommendations in this book will resonate. Scott makes it clear that pharmaceutical sales is ever evolving and those who plan to survive and thrive must become well rounded business people who bring value to their customers. Filled with both practical information and insight, Scott's book is an enjoyable and informative read!"

Phil Cramer

Region Business Director, Depomed

"Having worked in the Pharmaceutical Industry for 33 years as a field based representative with a wide variety of management roles, I read Mr. Costin's book with great interest. This is a candid and accurate assessment of the healthcare marketplace and pharma's ever changing role in that market. There are many real-world teachings and suggestions that have a practical application for field based organizations. It is a must read for both representatives and management."

Bill Proby

Retired after 33 years of Pharmaceutical Sales and Leadership experience

THE DOCTOR WON'T SEE YOU NOW

BE THE SAVVY, SUCCESSFUL BIOPHARMA REPRESENTATIVE

IN A RAPIDLY CHANGING INDUSTRY

Scott Costin

The Doctor Won't See You Know: Be the Savvy Biopharma Rep in a Rapidly Changing Industry
First Edition Trade Book, 2017

To order additional books go to www.thedoctorwontseeyounow.com

ISBN: 978-0-9978713-0-2

E-book also available

Editorial & Book Packaging: Inspira Literary Solutions, Gig Harbor, WA
Print Management: Scribe Book Company, Nashville, TN
Book Design: Brianna Showalter, Ruston, WA
Printed in the USA by Bookmasters

For Kristen, Taylor, and Jordan,
my patient and loving family.

CONTENTS

ACKNOWLEDGMENTS

For 26 years, my beautiful bride Kristen has supported me. When we moved to subzero South Dakota, football-fanatic Alabama, the central California coast, Seattle, eastern Pennsylvania, and back to Washington, it was all for my work. She sacrificed more than I ever knew and supported me always. For her and our two sons, Taylor and Jordan, my gratitude and love are endless.

Sincere thanks to my leaders: to my dad, Richard, there for me always and still today. From the USAF – in the 4SLS: Jay, Eric, Dave R., John H., Rick; at OTS: Gerry, Kim and Blue; at the 44th: Dave W., and John H., from biopharma: Mel Brown; she connects and leads with her heart like few others; Jeff Kline, who understands the priority of culture and multiplies the talent in his group; and the Aventis leaders who recognized some potential in my early work.

To Mindi, Kevin, Katy, Sheri, Jon and Dave – your achievements were extraordinary.

To my Pacific Northwest colleagues from the early days whose talent, intellect, and savvy elevated my work and perpetuated means to enjoy the challenges: Kirk Karste, Stephan Prechtel, Maristelle Tolentino, John Eddy, and Wendi Larson who taught me much as a new representative; more as a rookie manager. To Carmen Hall, who elevated my game in the field and the political home office.

My sincere gratitude to Arlyn Lawrence, her editing prowess, and her highly skilled, talented, and creative Inspiralit team.

Finally, to the one who never leaves my side, especially during the toughest times—thank you, God.

PREFACE

If you're still lucky enough to be in an accessible market or specialty, don't expect that will last.

Pratap Khedkar, Managing Principle – ZS Associates

Early in 1999, my wife and I were enjoying life on the central coast of California. I was stationed at Vandenberg Air Force Base and approaching the end of another three-year assignment. My next move would likely have been to the Pentagon, had I not decided to depart active duty service and move into the next chapter of our lives. Now I would work for the first time, post-college, in the private sector. My resume had drawn offers from two employers. It was time to announce my choice to each hiring manager.

My first call was to the hiring manager from a biologic and pharmaceutical manufacturer, Paul, to decline his offer. His response was, "Scott, if you change your mind within the next 12 months, call me—you won't have to interview again." I found this statement both surprising and yet quite welcome, although in no way did it alter my decision at the time. Yet after only six months with my new employer, I placed a call back to Paul. Why so soon?

My learning curve at that first company was steep. The plant I worked in was in the throes of substantial turnover and significant culture change. Though this change was definitely for the better, it was a tumultuous, stressful, and exhausting period. I was getting burned out at a meteoric pace and, even with all my post-military adrenaline for overachievement, the pace was not sustainable. It was at this point in my life I really understood that exhaustion trumps stubbornness and realized I would find substantial relief in the humility awaiting me. So I listened to the little voice inside and called Paul.

Back then, in the late 1990s and early 2000s, the biopharma industry had a fair number of representatives whose ranks were increasing annually, and now I would be one of them. According to IMS Health, a company that assesses many attributes of the biopharmaceutical field, the number of biopharma representatives quadrupled from 1995–2004. It turns out I wasn't the only person interested in the field! I quickly surmised this was a desirable and, consequently, competitive career arena. All my research, natural interests to date, and introspection led me to one definite conclusion: it was likely a solid fit for me.

After completing my initial biopharma training (three months' worth), it was time to go meet my customers—the doctors and other health care providers in and around Everett, Washington. But the customer environment I encountered was quite dissimilar to that depicted by friends around the country who had entered the industry before me. The once wide open doors of many clinics were closing to biopharma vendors. These were the customers my leaders told me to meet with in order to grow my business. It seemed like a sound strategy, but . . . what physicians and mid-level providers would I meet with?

Fast forward to 2017. As of the writing of this book, I've been working in the biopharma industry for 17 years with most of those years spent working in the Pacific Northwest. I've also had periodic responsibility for some outlying Northwest and Western states like Utah, Montana, and northern California. I worked in the corporate office for two and a half years with one company, garnering experience as a Sales Trainer and also as a National Training Manager. I've served as a Vendor Representative, Field Trainer, Specialty District Manager, Hospital District Manager, and most recently as a Health System Manager, Government Account Specialist and, again, an Area (District) Manager. I've supported small-molecule pharmaceuticals and multiple large-molecule biologics. I've supported products "sold" via prescriptions written by a Health Care Provider (HCP), and buy-and-bill products where the HCP, clinic, or health system purchases product directly from the manufacturer. I achieved some distinction during these years in the form of national sales awards, culture and leadership awards and, most importantly, in the form of eight promotions to leadership positions in the field and corporate office.

Having the benefit of service with five different companies and breadth of experience in the field organization, I have a diverse perspective on several Metropolitan Statistical Areas (MSAs), products, company marketing strategies, and cultural philosophies that drive the sales organization of these companies. I've also collected and studied dozens of articles and books over the years on many subjects I'll address in this book. This research was done by virtue of necessity; I had to know what was happening in health care and in my market to understand what was keeping my customers awake at night—so I could, in some way, help them with my products and resources. The few customers I could meet with were going to have to be my basis for developing my business.

Rule #1 in sales is to listen to your customer. So I started "listening" by reading what they were reading. Five months into my biopharmaceutical sales career, I started with an article published by Dr. Ashley Wazana in the Journal of the American Medical Association (JAMA), one of the more prestigious academic journals. With the title, "Physicians and the Pharmaceutical Industry; Is a Gift Ever Just a Gift?" you might quickly surmise this paper's direction. The author concluded:

The present extent of physician-industry interactions appears to affect prescribing and professional behavior and should be further addressed at the level of policy and education.[1]

Numerous policy makers and educators were way ahead of him. This wasn't the first article of its kind—some had been looking at industry influence for many years, even decades. The author of another article, published in the *Canadian Medical Association Journal* (CMAJ) back in 1993 concluded:

Physicians are affected by their interactions with the pharmaceutical industry. Further research needs to be done in most cases to determine whether such interactions lead to more or less appropriate prescribing practices.[2]

Similar articles were also published in the 1980s, 1970s, and even as far back as 1961 when a paper entitled, "Selling Drugs by 'Educating' Physicians,"[3] was published in the *Journal of Medical Education.*

At the genesis of my biopharma work, this wave of opinion was only gaining momentum and was about to achieve critical mass, inspiring dramatic policy changes by the local doctor's office, the group medical practice, the health system, and even federal health systems. Very quickly, I learned this critical mass had already been achieved in one noteworthy market—mine.

It was in May of 2000 when I began my career in the biopharma industry as a manufacturer's (vendor's) representative. At the time, I was only remotely aware, thanks to the insights of the representative I was replacing, of how pivotal a point this was in the evolution of my new career field. The above-mentioned articles were just being published, exposing how the biopharma industry was influencing health care providers to select and prescribe treatments that perhaps in some instances were not the most appropriate therapies for a given patient.

Here's a policy excerpt I encountered almost immediately upon beginning my biopharma career, stating the position of a large clinic regarding its interactions with "pharmaceutical" vendors like me. It's not open to much interpretation, as seen in The Everett Clinic's "Pharmaceutical Sales Ban—Prescribing Based on Research, Not Marketing":

In 1998, The Everett Clinic was one of the first medical groups in the country to ban pharmaceutical companies from physician offices.

We believe that prescribing decisions should be based on scientific research and medical experience, not advertising and marketing.[4]

So my own territory—in the Pacific Northwest—was leading the way—one of the first medical groups in the country to ban pharmaceutical companies from physician offices. And that wave was only gaining power and size.

I recall another clinic in Everett with HCPs who were somewhat willing to meet with biopharma vendors when I started work in May of 2000. Their limited willingness to meet with me came to an abrupt conclusion within my first six months on the job. This practice was already taking root and gaining strength in the region for several years. Even before the Everett Clinic closed its doors to pharma reps, another northwest health system, Group Health Cooperative (GHC) closed its doors to the "drop-in" vendor. As of the writing of this book, GHC—an Integrated Delivery Network (IDN) consisting of hospitals, health care providers (HCPs), clinics, pharmacies, and insurance plans all under one roof—is being purchased by Kaiser, a system notorious for highly restrictive vendor policies.

The distaste some health systems have for any work with biopharma vendors seems only to have grown in scope, emphasis, and application since 1961. In talking with a pharmacist from Group Health Cooperative (GHC), I learned she did not want patients to obtain access to patient savings information because she feared it would open the door to biopharma companies marketing directly to patients. This could possibly motivate the patient to ask his or her doctor to prescribe a more expensive, and perhaps no more efficacious or safe option than what GHC was recommending. This is only one example of the deeply rooted aversion some health systems have to working with, or even conversing with, biopharma representatives. And the doors keep closing. Pratap Khedkar of ZS Associates, a firm providing sales and marketing consulting mostly for the biopharma industry, stated in their 2015 AccessMonitor™

Executive Summary: "If you're still lucky enough to be in an accessible market or specialty, don't expect that will last. All the survey data points in the same direction, downward, and five years from now, you'll be in trouble."[5]

That's why the industry needs a book like this. We, as the biopharma industry, need to earn back the trust of our customers. We must provide genuine value via the means and at the frequency they prefer. We must ultimately reframe how we develop business, evolving to genuinely customer-centric strategies so we might engage in mutually beneficial business development with our customers.

In this book, I'll provide insight into why HCPs no longer want to meet with biopharma representatives as they once did, particularly in markets dominated by health systems. I'll also explore why it's important to understand the culture of a company, as well as the products and services it provides to customers. Then we may discern success plausibility in our own individual markets. You'll understand key skills and techniques for communicating with customers and getting an in-person meeting. We'll review techniques for assessing and aligning the resources you offer and for planning that all-important first meeting. I intend to provide you the basic understanding, tools, and strategies that will help us be successful while restoring credibility and trustworthiness to our industry one representative and one company at a time.

At the end of our time together, it's my sincere hope we as an industry will work to earn back the trust that has been decimated over the last three decades (e.g., think Vioxx®, Avandia®, and Neurontin®). Trust is earned one day, one event, and one person at a time and doesn't come quickly or easily. However, it is essential for the long-term success of our industry. Success, in our capitalist culture, will always be defined by constantly increasing shareholder value, but that value must be achieved through ethical and patient-centered means.

For this trust to be earned, we can't merely be prototypical reps; we must be savvy biopharma representatives. Dictionary.

com defines "savvy" (adj.) as, "shrewdly informed; experienced and well-informed; canny."[6] This accurately characterizes a few of the most fundamental attributes necessary for our success. The savvy biopharma vendor is focused on positive patient outcomes. He or she is skilled, constantly learning, well-versed in the interests of the customer, and assertive at integrating street smarts and business development ideas when collaborating with business development and marketing leaders. Not only that, he or she is voracious in the study of markets and products, and adherent to the policies, rules, and regulations that define the lines within which we all must remain.

You, the biopharma vendor, work in the trenches where many fear to tread. Excelling down here is a great achievement, where street smarts often trump book smarts, and how you say just one word can make or break your business—or, worse, a patient's outcome. You are on the front line, executing the plans, sometimes making breakthroughs, and sometimes taking the bullets. You know what works and you know what doesn't work.

You can be tremendously valuable to your customers with the work you do. You can make a significant positive impact. You are the ones doing the hard work face-to-face with those you value the most: your customers. You are the men and women in the arena. This book is for you.

It is not the critic who counts; not the man who points out how the strong man stumbles, or where the doer of deeds could have done them better. The credit belongs to the man who is actually in the arena, whose face is marred by dust and sweat and blood; who strives valiantly; who errs, who comes short again and again, because there is no effort without error and shortcoming; but who does actually strive to do the deeds; who knows great enthusiasms, the great devotions; who spends himself in a worthy cause; who at the best knows in the end the triumph of high achievement, and who at the worst, if he fails, at least fails while daring greatly, so that his place shall never be with those cold and timid souls who neither know victory nor defeat.

– Theodore Roosevelt, 1910[7]

Scott Costin
May 2017

INTRODUCTION

"Silence like a cancer grows."
- Paul Simon[1]

Rob Reiner's 1995 film, *The American President,*[2] demonstrated well the consequences of not speaking so you are heard; of not being a bold leader. The fictional film takes place during an election year, and the presidential challenger, Bob Rumson, is doing all the talking—he dominates the chatter in the media. Consequently, he begins to sway public opinion in his favor and against the President (played by Michael Douglas).

The President is adamant—he will not stoop to the level of the challenger's rhetoric, which is negative and sometimes personal. An advisor to the first family (played by Michael J. Fox) helps the President push back, encouraging tenacity and providing direction. He tells his boss, "Bob Rumson is the only one doing the talking! People want leadership, Mr. President! And in the absence of genuine leadership, they'll listen to anyone who steps up to the microphone. They want leadership." I believe we have a similar situation in the biopharma industry.

Most American citizens have probably heard about the Martin Shkreli scandal. In 2015, Shkreli—CEO of Turing Pharmaceuticals—dramatically raised the price of a life-saving anti-parasitic agent called pyrimethamine (Daraprim). Pyrimethamine is used to treat patients with HIV/AIDS or those with decreased immune function, such as cancer patients.[3] In the blink of an eye, he raised the price 5,556%, from $13.50 to $750 per tablet.[4]

The headlines quickly followed, alerting the public to this aggressive insult not only to patients but to the entire health care system. In short order, journalists who were writing about drug pricing were reinvigorated. Egregious pharmaceutical pricing headlines abounded. You see, this is how it works: media outlets print/show/discuss subjects that generate ratings. Good ratings generate revenue. Revenue generates profit. The journalists were hooked because the public was buying it. They churned out:

- "Was Turing Pharmaceuticals' 5000% Price Increase a Tipping Point?" *Health News Review*, October, 2015[5]
- "Doctors, Hospitals Condemn Out-of-Control Drug Prices as Senate Investigation Begins," *Washington Post,* December, 2015[6]
- "Senators Condemn Big Price Increases for Drugs." *New York Times,* December, 2015[7]
- "Drugmakers Raise Prices Despite Criticisms," *Wall Street Journal,* January, 2016[8]

Once again, it appeared the public wanted a target on the reviled pharmaceutical industry and found an easy one in Mr. Shkreli. He accurately represented the entire industry, right? Didn't all those shareholder-value-driven CEOs say, "Stick it to the patient so we can make more money?"

Not at all. Martin Shkreli is not in any way a proper representation of the aggregate biopharma industry. His actions were despicable. Nonetheless, the public latched on to this vile behavior as representing the biopharma masses despite the fact that, in all actuality, healthy and honorable companies do exist in biopharma, perhaps in numbers greater than many perceive.

Very soon after Shkreli thrust himself onto the national stage with one epic overnight price increase, Imprimis Pharmaceuticals found a noble business opportunity. They would provide a compounded formulation of pyrimethamine in combination with leucovorin (a drug with which pyrimethamine is commonly prescribed) at 99 dollars for a 100-tablet bottle. Well done, Imprimis. Alas, the headlines persisted, scolding the entire industry on pricing practices. Ask the public what's better known to them: Martin Shkreli or Imprimis. My suspicion is Imprimis will be an unknown to most.

Are those headlines really warranted? Probably not. There are, however, many more reasons to question the seemingly voracious media appetite for pharma-bashing topics. Does the general public understand the genuine value the biopharma industry provides the healthcare system? What does the lay press communicate to the masses around the biopharma (pharmaceutical) industry? In my research, it's generally not favorable. So how bad is this industry, really?

According to *Cancer Statistics 2015,* "Over the past two decades there has been a steady decline in the cancer death rate as a result of fewer Americans smoking and advances in cancer prevention, early detection, and treatment." Moreover, earlier in the article the authors stated that using drugs like Imatinib* doubled survival rates for patients with chronic myeloid leukemia "from 31% in the early 1990s to 60% in 2004-2010."[9]

Facts like this—the positive, the reason for optimism, the anti-Shkreli—are in short supply in the lay press. And yet, if you ask someone whose father, mother, sister, or brother is alive today thanks (in part) to a particular therapy, you'll get much more than a simple headline extolling the merits of medicines. You may just get happy tears.

Have you ever heard of the death sentence called Hepatitis C? There will likely be a day when it's only a remote memory to a few. That's thanks to Pharmasset and Gilead, the latter being the manufacturer of Harvoni™. They market it—a combination of sofosbuvir (Sovaldi) and ledipasvir—to treat chronic Hepatitis C genotypes 1, 4, 5, and 6, as well as patients co-infected by HIV (as of November

---

* Marketed by Novartis as Gleevec in the US, this is a tyrosine-kinase inhibitor used to treat several cancer types.

12, 2015).[10] Studies indicate Harvoni™ cures most of these patients in just a few months.

Gilead has taken a beating from some for their pricing of the medication; $94,500 for a course of treatment.[11] However, a *Washington Post* article co-authored by ProPublica—an independent, non-profit organization serving the public interest through investigative journalism—took a different stance. It cited, "The new Hepatitis C drugs have a higher cure rate – 90% or higher – than previous treatments, as well as fewer harmful side effects. Some studies have shown, despite their price tag, the drugs justify their cost based on the better quality of life they provide and the health expenses that patients avoid in the future."[12]

I have a friend whose mother is now free from Hepatitis C. I asked him if it was worth the price to his mother and the health care system (since she's covered by the state's Medicaid insurance). His response? "The only reason my mom is now alive and healthy is that medicine; she's cured of the insidious disease she'd had for years that was going to kill her."

How many bacterial infections, once fatal, are now cured because antibiotics can help our bodies win the battle? How many potentially deadly cardiovascular events were averted thanks to antihypertensive therapies? How many diseases like polio are largely distant memories thanks to vaccines? Yet, in the minds of the public, these health benefits—courtesy of biopharma research, development, manufacturing, and distribution—are rarely discussed in the press.

Perhaps it really is the cost. Why are these new medicines so expensive? Do we spend such an exorbitant amount of money on biopharma therapies as a percentage of health care spending that the value of biopharma is overinflated? Are these curative and preventive therapies so ridiculously overpriced we should be embarrassed to even mention the subject? The answer is an unequivocal no.

According to the Centers for Disease Control and Prevention

(CDC), the percent of national health expenditures for prescription drugs in 2013 was 9.3%, similar to what it was in previous years. In contrast, the percentage of national health expenditures for hospital care in 2013 was 32% and for physician and clinical services it was 20%.[13] When prescribed and administered appropriately—or better yet, optimally—biopharma therapies can provide significant benefit and value to the patients, the clinics, and the health systems that treat them, at an appropriate price. Unfortunately, this truth hasn't been communicated very well to the public or to our individual customers. Couple this fact with much of what you'll read in Chapter One, and it's not hard to understand why health care providers and their leaders, residents, fellows, pharmacists, and even medical students don't want to meet with biopharma representatives nearly as often as they did just 10 to 20 years ago.

Recently, I spoke with an executive at a large biopharma manufacturer. He is a successful, bright, and pragmatic businessperson. I asked him why biopharma does so little to promote the genuine value it provides to patients and the overall health care system of the United States. We discussed PhRMA, the Pharmaceutical Research and Manufacturer's Association, a large industry trade group, and he said this isn't really the group to take the helm on this subject. So I dug a bit more and found there are organizations doing some work in this area already. Still, opportunities abound. The biopharma industry may find significance and value in promoting the benefits of our work to the public. Taking just a few steps to demonstrate the value we provide to the aggregate health care system and to patients may now be warranted.

Making that statement is a bit of a risk. Yet as someone who has spent over 17 years working with healthy companies that manufacture products of substantive value, I know I can say it with confidence in its accuracy. In the words of Steve Wozniak, from the 2015 movie *Steve Jobs*, "It's not binary. You can be decent and gifted at the same time."[14]

Biopharma has products that are "gifted." They are of definite, substantive, and sometimes even immeasurable worth to patients and health systems. Some companies are also decent with their products. They provide genuine and functional value ethically, honorably, and profitably to the customers they serve and the patients treated by those customers. It doesn't have to be one or the other—the business of biopharma doesn't have to be binary, and in many instances it isn't. Ask someone who is free from cancer or someone who is free from Hepatitis C. Talk to someone who is free from pneumonia or free from parasites thanks to Imprimis' leadership with their compounded pyrimethamine at a dollar per dose. Ask them, "Was the therapy worth the price?" They will certainly tell you. And if they don't, their families and friends will.

Although biopharma provides tremendous benefits to health systems and patients, we don't show it well. I hope the proceeding pages will help all of us make even greater contributions to our customers and the health systems for which many of them work. Most importantly, I hope these pages help us find honorable success in a perhaps poorly perceived yet profoundly valuable industry that ultimately exists to serve just one person: the patient.

1
Access Denied

We try never to forget that medicine is for the people. It is not for profits. The profits follow, and if we have remembered that, they never fail to appear. The better we have remembered it, the larger they have been.

—George Merck[1]

You're a new biopharma representative and your training is complete. You are three months into your new role and ready to begin developing the business in your own territory. All you need to begin building your reputation of success are enthusiasm, business development knowledge, informational and material resources, and a plan to meet with seven physicians on day one.

You arrive at the first clinic of the day and assemble your plan. You greet the receptionist, identify yourself, and indicate your reason for wanting to meet with the doctor. The gatekeeper firmly and professionally informs you, "Sorry, they don't meet with reps."

After a few more minutes of attempting to find some modicum of hope to talk with or at least leave some information for one or more of the HCPs, you finally acknowledge the environment you are in, thank the receptionist, leave a business card (promptly deposited as refuse), and depart. You confirmed what you already suspected: This was a "no access" clinic.

Office #2 produces a similar encounter.

At Office #3, the gatekeeper takes your business card back; you see a ray of hope and feel a twinge of excitement. He returns moments later to inform you the nurse practitioner has no interest in meeting but thanks you for stopping by.

The day's fourth clinic produces a different response from the receptionist: "We're not permitted to meet with reps—in fact you're not even allowed in here."

"But I have a product that your doctors will want to know about," you appeal. "May I at least leave some information for the docs?"

"The doctors get their information from other sources—I'm sorry, but you can't leave anything."

So what's the big deal? A couple clinics closed their doors to you. So what? You're a vendor. Make some cold calls. Get on the phone and generate some leads. There are more HCPs in your territory. Find them and get to them.

Such suggestions are fundamental expectations of many sales programs. However, biopharma typically has one foundational metric that must be achieved regardless of the market in which a representative works. The metric is defined as "calls per day," also known as "frequency." This refers to the number of HCPs a representative meets with on a given business day. A typical target is seven to nine meetings per day. These interactions are often defined as the foundation for a representative's potential impact on a health care provider, health system, and overall territory business development.

By now, you can surely see a crack in this foundation. Doctors, clinics, groups, and systems are closing their doors to biopharma. It's challenging to communicate with physicians when they are behind doors of institutions with conflict of interest policies, vendor management policies, and anti-influence cultures restricting vendor access.

The biopharma industry developed and enforced an expectation of achieving "call frequency" goals because they generated results—very good results. Talk with more doctors more frequently and you'll achieve better results than your peers. Year after year, the most successful reps and leaders in the country would stand on stage at national sales meetings and say, "Instead of going home at 5:00 p.m., I made just one more call per day." That approach worked much more successfully when the industry was less regulated, fewer restrictions were levied on us, and HCPs and leaders were more readily accessible than today.

Given this challenge, it's helpful to understand why this metric was established and is still being enforced even when some data indicate thousands of calls planned by commercial organizations cannot be executed due to restricted HCP access.[2]

Come on—How Bad Is Access, Really?

Let's begin by peering into some operational limitations experienced by the field force at Abell Pharma.*

Abell was growing. The FDA had recently approved Abell's new product. Consequently, consultants told Abell's sales and marketing leadership they needed to increase their field sales force so they could: a) achieve their call frequency targets, and b) achieve their sales targets. The former, of course, in large part determined the latter.

The opportunity at Abell caught the attention of Roy Thomas. Abell was a smaller organization, which Roy thought would be nimble and adaptable to local market dynamics. This was a top priority for him and any team he would lead given the number of HCPs who had become almost completely inaccessible in his markets.

---

* This picture is drawn from a composite of pharma manufacturers with whom I have had various forms of contact; the composite picture I have drawn here does not represent any one company.

Roy joined Abell and had his team in place within a few months. Optimism and enthusiasm reigned supreme, as they were launching a novel therapy that company executives were certain would generate hundreds of millions in sales in its first years. They were doomed before they opened their first training module.

Roy's team was provided a list of HCPs on which to call—that is, attempt to meet with. Anyone who knows the Minnesota market knows it is one with very limited access to HCPs. Roy's team started working to meet with their "targeted" HCPs with two representatives sharing the greater Minneapolis/St. Paul market. The depth of their peril is underscored by the research two of his representatives conducted over a period of several weeks.

Representative A, whom I'll call Rich, had just over 1,000 HCPs working in his territory; 500 of those were prescribers of medications that made them a priority for Rich. From that list of 500, Rich was tasked with identifying 100 HCPs he would meet with regularly throughout the year. After knocking on many doors, making hundreds of phone calls, and reading dozens of policies, Rich concluded the following: realistically, he could expect to meet with 17 HCPs in a given month. At seven calls per day, that meant he had about two and a half days of work per month. Abell was not getting everything it could from its well-educated, talented, experienced, and motivated representative.

Then there was Representative B, whom I'll call Kristen. Her territory was also in the Minneapolis/St. Paul area. Kristen also had approximately 1,000 health care providers in her territory, with approximately 500 having prescribed medications similar to those Kristen would be representing. Kristen was also deliberate in her door knocking and phone calling. But in the end, Kristen had just 11 HCPs she could realistically expect to see in a given month. What would Kristen do with all her free time? Talking with the expected seven HCPs per day, she would be finished meeting customers after the second business day of any given month.

These territory characteristics were not unique to the Minneapolis/St. Paul market or even to the state. Other Abell colleagues in Wisconsin, Washington, Oregon, and Boston were experiencing similar challenges, as evidenced in the national business (sales) rankings. During the years Roy worked at Abell, the district managers working in the markets with notoriously restricted access consistently performed poorly when ranked against their peers. This continued year after year after year.

Roy's story is one I've seen several colleagues and friends endure. A challenge of every manager in like markets is generating levels of business similar to markets with substantially greater access to customers (just one varying dynamic). And the challenge for managers and representatives with better access to HCPs today is this: access enjoyed today is not expected to endure.[3]

The Trend Toward Restricting HCP Access

You may perhaps be asking yourself if the circumstances described here are isolated or perhaps insignificant—fair questions indeed. Thankfully, there are respected data substantiating these claims.

Many companies support the commercial groups of biopharma manufacturers with information used to build and deploy a field force. One such company is ZS Associates; one of their tools is called AccessMonitor™. This tool identifies market attributes, such as the number of physicians a representative can expect to see over a given period of time. The tool also identifies several subsets of data, such as the number of specialists or primary care physicians who will permit best-in-class representatives to call on them X number of times per year.

In the 2014 Executive Summary of AccessMonitor™, Pratap Khedkar—Managing Principal at ZS Associates, Philadelphia—reported, "The access problem doesn't seem to have bottomed out in certain areas, even where access was already poor." ZS Associates defines markets using the term Metropolitan Statistical Areas or

MSAs. The five most restrictive access MSAs are:

1. Minneapolis/St. Paul, Minnesota (most restricted access market in the country)
2. Milwaukee, Wisconsin
3. Seattle, Washington
4. Boston, Massachusetts
5. Portland, Oregon

Note that in all five MSAs, the "access" became more restrictive between 2013 and 2014. The ZS AccessMonitor™ website states, "51% of physicians are considered accessible in 2014, compared to 55% in 2013 and 65% in 2012."[4]

As you review the proceeding two tables you continue to feel how bleak the outlook on access appears. The first table is from ZS Associates' 2011 data set on physician access. The second represents their 2015 data set. Notably, this trend toward decreased access is no longer isolated to a few MSAs. It's growing as health systems identify reasons to limit representative communication with their employees. It is now the dominant culture in many health systems, starting back in the 1990s with groups like The Everett Clinic. And they publicly displayed the results of their policy change prohibiting pharmaceutical representatives from marketing to their HCPs.

FIGURE. Sales representative access limits for the United States by Metropolitan Statistical Area (MSA) for semester (S1) 2011. The map comes from the S1 2011 AccessMonitor™ report produced by ZS Associates. Among MSAs noted to have severe access restrictions, 20% or more of prescribers within such locations have severe access restrictions according to S1 2011 data contained in AccessMonitor™ from ZS Associates. Access measured at the MSA level as percentage of prescribers rated with an AccessMonitor™ "no-see rating" between 1 and 5. Non-MSA geographic areas are noted in white. Variations also exist in physician access by specialty expressed as percentage of prescribers for S1 2011, ranked by "Severe Access Restrictions" and organized by little or no access, moderate access, and severe access restrictions by AccessMonitor™ no-see ratings of 8 to 10, 4 to 7, and 1 to 3, respectively. (This Figure is adapted from ZS Associates 2015 data set depicting access to physicians.)

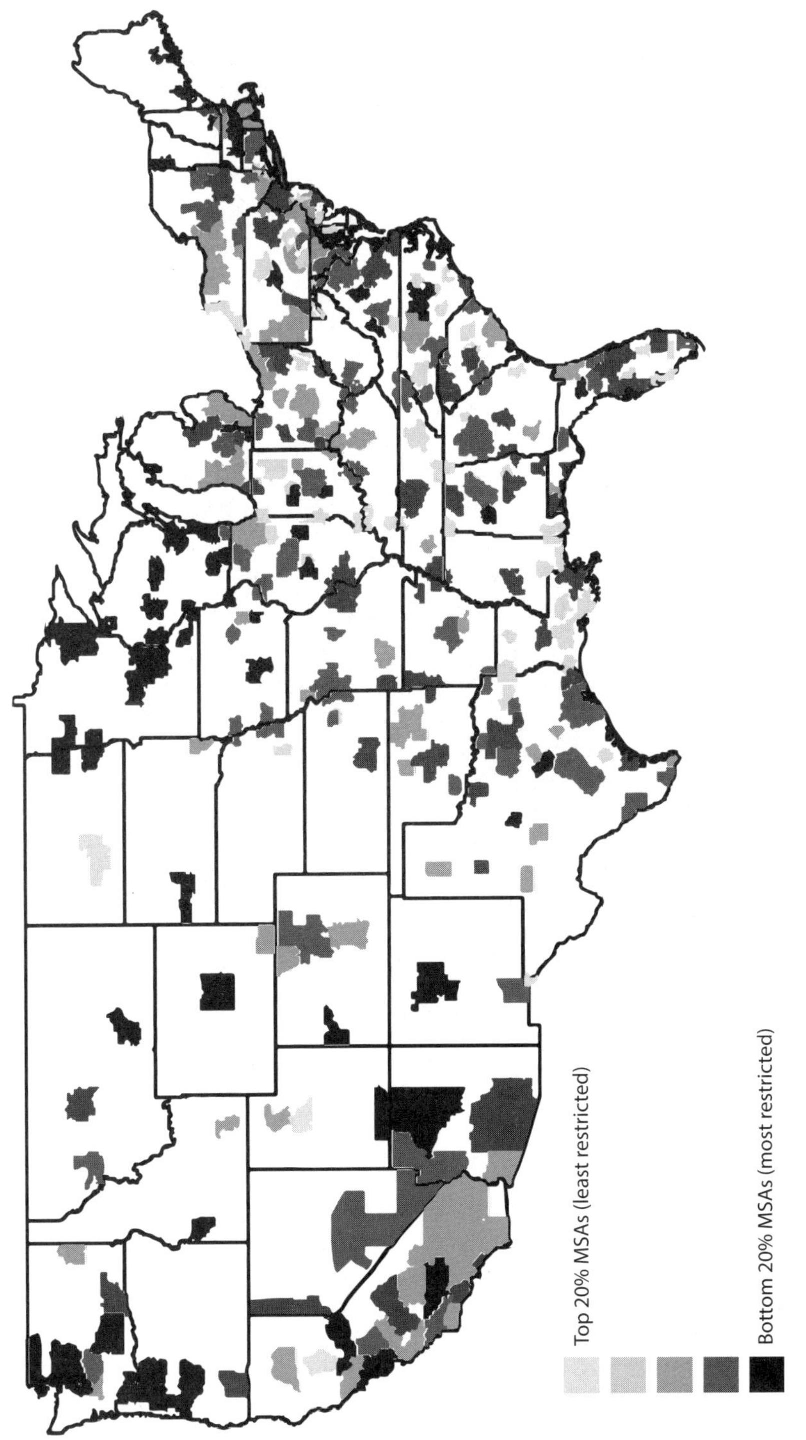
Top 20% MSAs (least restricted)
Bottom 20% MSAs (most restricted)

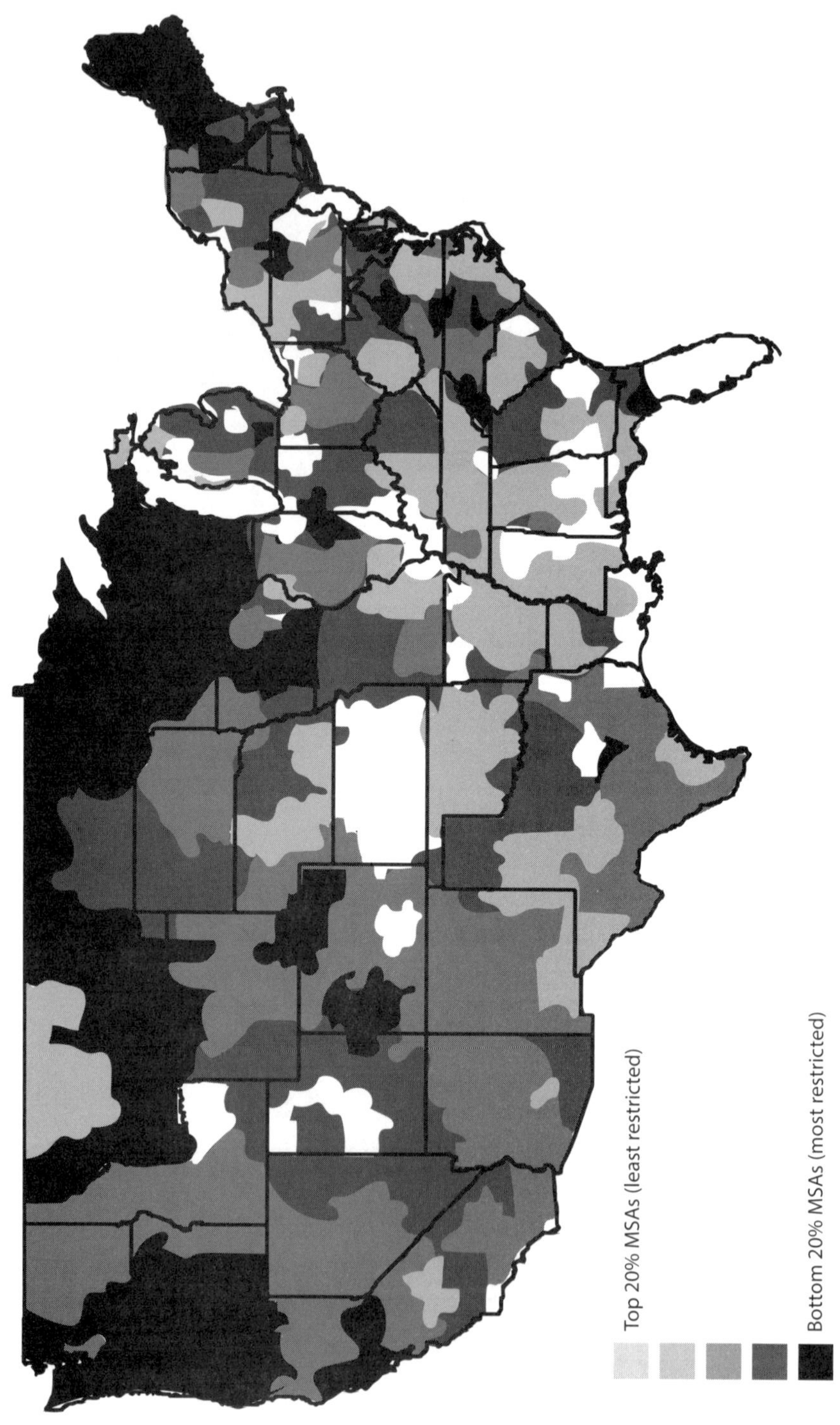
Top 20% MSAs (least restricted)
Bottom 20% MSAs (most restricted)

Not long after The Everett Clinic HCPs were largely cut off from communicating with biopharma representatives, clinic leadership noticed a change. They reduced their drug spend by 10% after they "banned sales reps and samples in 1998."[5] The 10% savings they enjoyed was contrasted by costs increasing 15% in other group practices similar to The Everett Clinic according to Dr. Fisk, a leader in the health care landscape. The Everett Clinic is far from alone in this procedural and cultural change.

Similar "influence free" policies—such as the policy in place since 2007 at the Henry Ford Health System in Detroit, Michigan—not only continue to be implemented but also hailed as revolutionary solutions to some of the many challenges facing health systems. The policies prohibit gifts, food, or samples to employees within the system's seven hospitals and 27 clinics. Dr. Kathleen Yaremchuk, head of clinical practice at Henry Ford, stated in 2009 that one consequence of the policy to this health system was "freed up time equal to employing eight more doctors."

Dr. Yaremchuk went on to state, "We gave them [doctors] time."[6] It might be difficult to find something to provide your doctors more valuable than time, especially in today's hurried world of health care. Dr. Yaremchuck lectures on this subject nationally, so the story of this system's success with limiting influence is being propagated. Today the movement to limit industry influence continues its rapid expansion into almost every market in the country.

Note in what you just read: both systems not only restricted reps; they also banned samples. In so doing, system administrators took away a valuable incentive HCPs had to meet with industry: the sample medications reps often left with physicians.

These group practices had another noteworthy attribute that led administrators to minimize the time HCPs spent with vendors: HCP productivity. Time talking to vendors was time not spent in an exam room, charting, or talking with a colleague about a referral or lab results for a particular patient. In some administrators' minds, vendor representatives were inhibiting productivity and that inhibited revenue.

Today, this anti-influence culture and the rationale for it are infused into doctors at the beginning of their training. The American Medical Student's Association (AMSA), partnering with the Pew Prescription Project, assembled a scorecard. The intent is to objectively evaluate the effectiveness of the country's medical schools at limiting influence on doctors from industry. The Pew Charitable Trusts also assembled a document entitled "Best Practices to Eliminate or Reduce Conflicts of Interest at Academic Medical Centers." This document outlines several specific requirements, such as required "conflict of interest" training, no-sample policies, no food accepted, no gifts of any type, no remuneration from speaking promotionally for industry, and no attendance at promotional events by industry.[7] These are not isolated policies. There are many groups like AMSA and the Pew Trusts continually advocating for these and other steps to reduce biopharma influence on clinicians' therapeutic decisions.

The Depth of This Culture Shift

Some time ago, I visited a specialty clinic within the federal health care system. During an in-service training session, I'd met most of the attending physicians, residents, and the medical students associated with the department's medical training program. I did most of my regular communicating with this group through their residency coordinator.

Subsequent to the in-service, however, my time with the providers was limited at best seeing them only in passing in the hallway while stocking their library of patient information or at the front desk while talking with a nurse. Knowing a fair amount about the interests of some doctors in the clinic, I was fairly certain two physicians in particular would be interested in a new training resource recently made available to my customers and me. I approached Matt, one of two clinic receptionists, and asked if he would mind bringing something to these docs and see if they had a minute to talk about this training opportunity. Matt resisted, saying, "I probably shouldn't bother them—they both just finished seeing patients for the morning."

I persisted, "Both of these docs expressed interest in this type of information when I provided the in-service training a few months back; I think they might be interested and I can provide them some details briefly now if they're available."

Then Matt made things clear for me (with genuine kindness, I should add). "Scott, you don't understand. If I were to go back there and present them with what you're asking me to give them, they'll be angry with me. For me to do this, I'd be putting my job at risk because I'm not permitted to do it." His HCPs rarely spoke with vendors; this was quite intentional. And this "anti-influence" culture has intensified over the last 17 years.

After many years of this work, much research, and thousands of conversations with hundreds of HCPs, staff, and health care leaders, I understand their perspective fairly well. Doctors, pharmacists. and leaders of health systems and group clinics often pride themselves on unbiased decision-making. They often resist biopharma industry influence in any form. Any perceived relationship to biopharma can diminish physicians' credibility in the eyes of their peers. In academic medicine, peer pressure has proven a powerful deterrent to staff forming relationships with industry.

During a meeting with an academic physician in the summer of 2015, she thanked me for some recent training I had provided her and her colleagues. She went on to tell me how vendors were not merely kept at arm's length in this facility, they were shunned. If a doctor met with one she'd be questioned—no, challenged—by her colleagues.

"Scott, last time I met with you here, one of the other physicians asked me why I was talking with you. I had to explain myself, which I did. I appreciate your help and will continue to ask for it, but that is the mentality here."

This needs to sink in for a minute or two. The feelings of this physician and the academic health system for which she works are not isolated. This story exemplifies for me how powerful the aversion can be to any affiliation or perceived influence by industry; it is deeply rooted. In fact, the HCPs in this clinic rarely meet with vendors if they meet with them at all. The customers I support tell me they rarely, very rarely, talk with representatives of biopharma or any vendors for that matter.

This federal specialty clinic I mentioned earlier had two in-service training meetings with vendors in 2014. One was with me. That was a grand total of two substantive meetings with biopharma vendors in all of 2014. In 2015, they had none.

Back to Abell Pharma

The average number of HCPs each member of Roy's team could reasonably expect to meet with during any given month was about one-third the number they were expected to see. Roy's team had to work three times as fast, three times as hard, and three times as much as the more open-access territories in the country. He and his team (expectedly) found this to be physically impossible.

Roy's representatives applied themselves vigorously every day to get to their customers by any means possible. They levied all their talent, experience, skill, and energy to talk with some customers—not just the highest priority customers but *any* appropriate customers. They experienced some success by applying their talents and also by applying some skills Roy taught them. Unfortunately, it wasn't enough to sustain many of them. Six months in, two reps gave Roy their notice. Within the next two years, two more resigned.

If we were talking about baseball, we could say Roy had been hired to help his team win the most games in a single season, year after year.* Given the limited access his team had to their customers,

* Currently this record is held by the 2001 Seattle Mariners and the 1906 Chicago Cubs, each with 116 wins that season.

Roy and his team had the chance to bat only three innings per game versus the nine innings most other teams enjoyed. With roughly 220 "games" (work days) per year and only three innings of offense per game, he and his team had absolutely no chance at winning the most games in a year.

The opportunity for some business growth was there. His team could help some accessible customers and they did grow business. But the territories around the country with the best growth were often those with the most doctors a team could meet with. Year after year, there was a discernable and direct correlation between the two. Unfortunately for the majority of representatives in the territories with low access to customers, the results were consistently poor. Unfortunately for Abell's leaders, the consequences included high turnover of valuable talent.

Even more important, patients who may have benefitted from Abell's product perhaps experienced that benefit less frequently. The value the company provided to its representatives and managers in the form of resources was not substantive enough for most customers to warrant work with the representatives. And herein lies a critical variable in this equation: the *genuine value* customers derive from biopharma manufacturers and our representatives.

Do We Provide Value?

The reality is that, for all the aversion of medical students, academia, and some policy makers, we have products and information that can be extremely helpful to patients, HCPs, and their employers. I'll address the concept of genuine value in greater detail later. For now, here's a snapshot of what value looks like to one HCP.

Just yesterday, I spoke with a physician employed by a mid-sized, non-academic health system. After 23 years in practice as an internist, he concluded physicians practicing in closed-access systems understand less than he and his colleagues do about newer therapies, because he and his colleagues do talk with vendors occasionally. With vendor representatives, he controls the conversations and assesses the information provided often conducting his own research as well. In so doing, he has a firm conviction that his strategy is sound and ultimately helpful to his patients.

Notably, even with this philosophy, he won't touch a new therapy for at least a year after it is introduced to him. As well, in subsequent visits by the reps, he doesn't permit them to do any more than greet him, obtain a signature for samples, say thank you, and depart. He has what he needs from them. He finds a smattering of value, but after initial product introduction that value is largely in the form of samples.

Yet samples cannot be relied on as the primary value representatives offer because more and more systems are prohibiting accepting samples. There has to be more substance to our value, or we simply become minimally relevant or even burdensome through our inquiries or meeting requests.

Build a great product and they will come? In today's climate, they'll only come if you go out and connect with them. With or without genuine value to provide customers, we are obliged by our employers to effectively develop our business through appropriate use of our products by patients in our markets. This requires us to communicate with and support our customers—the HCPs in our MSAs. However, their aversion to communicating with vendors can make our work quite challenging. In several instances it's not just an aversion; it's policy.

I spoke with a new friend recently. She's an oncologist with a local health system. When she started her work with this group she was told she could no longer speak for the biopharma industry and was no longer permitted to meet with any vendor representatives. She was completely cut off by her employer's policy. When we work to meet with some customers we may be asking these customers to violate their own policies! *What have we done to ourselves?*

To better understand the perspective of the prescribers, clinics, and health systems directing patients to use our therapies, it's helpful to comprehend the numerous events that compounded to help motivate this aversion. What was perceived as value in years past is often no longer provided by the industry. Payers exert far greater control over therapeutic options and decisions made by HCPs and their employers. Insurers continue raising premiums and increasing costs patients pay out-of-pocket. Legislation enhances financial incentives for health systems to aggregate and grow in size (and consequent patient volume). Myriad industries and legislators impact the costs and quality of care we pay for.

Biopharma is one significant entity in this market. To understand what genuine value is to our customers in the health care system, we need to understand their priorities and interests and the priorities and interests of their customers. Then we can develop and align our resources with those priorities, interests, and needs to help them achieve their objectives.

2
What Happened?

Don't ever take a fence down until
you know why it was put up.
—Robert Frost[1]

During my teen years, a lament of mine to my parents was, "You don't trust me!" Looking back, their rationale for distrust was sound. I didn't earn it. I said I'd be home by 9:00 p.m., or told them I'd notify them before my friends and I hiked into the woods to fish at some remote pond. I'd forget—and roll in around 10:00 p.m. to find worried parents. And then I expected them to trust me? I hadn't completed the simplest tasks they'd asked of me; why would they possibly believe I'd be responsible with the family car? (My learning curve was steep there as well.)

Put these minor examples into the larger context of conscious deception perpetrated by a multi-national biopharma corporation that willfully minimizes safety data from doctors,[2] incurs billions of dollars in fines from the Department of Justice for inappropriate sales and marketing practices,[3] and is known to rarely inform physicians about serious adverse events associated with a therapy.[4] One should have little difficulty discerning why physicians may be skeptical of any information presented by an industry representative. Why would a doctor want to meet with 10 vendors per day? Or even one?

Think back to when Vioxx® became a household name in 2004. Perhaps it was because Dorothy Hamill marketed it on TV commercials placed by Merck, but more likely it was because it was widely prescribed and then withdrawn due to increased cardiac risk factors associated with its use. This seemingly chivalrous gesture was viewed by some as too little, too late. The ensuing investigations produced far graver facts. Investigators ultimately attributed tens of thousands of deaths to Vioxx®.[5]

More disturbing is the evidence now available showing that Merck scientists knew of the increased cardiac risk. Rather than present these findings, Merck appears to have sought to minimize and conceal them. The Merck research chief, Dr. Edward Scolnick, communicated in an email to colleagues on March 9, 2000 that cardiovascular events were "clearly there" and that this was a "shame."[6]

Sadly, as far back as November 21, 1996, a memo from a Merck official cited interest in conducting a trial to demonstrate safety of Vioxx®. However, to show the difference clearly, patients would not be allowed to take aspirin. The memo then stated: "There is a substantial chance that significantly higher rates" of cardiovascular problems would be seen in the Vioxx® group.[7] When Merck decided to withdraw Vioxx® from the US market in September 2004, chief executive Raymond Gilmartin said the study findings associating Vioxx® use with heart attack and stroke risk were "unexpected." Internal Merck documents showed they were quite expected.[8]

In another case, one of the largest fines ever levied to date against any corporation was incurred by a large biopharma manufacturer, Glaxo Smith Kline (GSK), in 2012. This fine amounted to $3 billion. GSK pleaded guilty to three criminal charges involving their drugs Paxil®, Avandia® and Wellbutrin®. The criminal fine associated with their actions involving these drugs was $1 billion. The other $2 billion was paid as part of a civil settlement addressing their sales and marketing practices around Advair®, a blockbuster asthma drug, and several other drugs.[9]

If that weren't enough, three additional biopharma manufacturers are included in the list of top 10 fines ever levied on corporations. As of 2014, the pharmaceutical industry's reputation in the eyes of the public was on par with tobacco companies and the financial sector.[10]

The settlements levied against Merck and GSK are but two examples. See for yourself: do some research on the settlements manufacturers were required to pay regarding these drugs Neurontin®, Actos®, Fen-Phen, Celexa®, Lexapro®, Accutane®, OxyContin®, Trileptal®, Depakote®, Rapamune®, NovoSeven®, Seroquel®, Vytorin®, Zyprexa®, and others. When you delve into the impact these incidents had on physicians' and healthcare leaders' perception of our industry, you see a clear result: credibility and trustworthiness lost.

Who is obliged to carry this reputation in front of customers every day? Who is in the arena every day? Who is in the trenches? You and me. The representatives bear this burden as we work diligently to earn the trust and respect of customers who often have a deep disdain for our role and the conduct of our industry. When we go to work every day, our success is predicated on being viewed as credible. (Credibility is defined as "offering reasonable grounds for being believed."[11]) Yet biopharma organizations have paid more than $13 billion since 2009 to resolve US Department of Justice allegations of fraudulent marketing practices with many major news outlets reporting on these large fines.[12] In that light, one can see how our credibility may perhaps be worthy of some skepticism.

Restoring credibility and our ability to provide resources of genuine value are foundational to building trust with customers. If we are not trusted, how are we to be effective? Some organizations deploying a field force invest so little in understanding the necessity of building trust with customers that I'm a bit surprised any vendors are permitted to speak with any HCP or leader. If we can restore our credibility and earn customer trust, we can effectively align our resources to their priorities and contribute significantly to them achieving optimal outcomes for their patients and their employers.

Jennifer Norton Wilson, clinical pharmacist for The Everett Clinic and for many years the sole contact for biopharma vendors, characterizes well the impact of our reduced credibility and trustworthiness on some health care leaders. "We were very aware that the pharma companies were pushing newer products." You now understand the promotion we engaged in didn't always turn out favorably for many. She continued, "In the long run, we decided that it would be better for our practice if we had less biased individuals providing information."[13] In the eyes of some like Jennifer and the CEO of The Everett Clinic, we damaged our credibility and trustworthiness to a point necessitating almost complete exclusion. However, times are changing. Thankfully, it appears we may be learning.

The US military likes to acknowledge the work and sacrifices of its men and women through awarding medals. Each medal is accompanied by a citation or brief explanation of the actions meriting the award. During my years of service, the final line of awarded medal citations generally read, "The actions of (rank and name) reflect great credit upon (himself or herself), and the United States Air Force." Biopharma representatives want to be able to say the same: "The actions of Representative Karste reflect great credit upon himself and the biopharma industry." For this opinion to manifest in our customers, we must be credible and trustworthy.

Thank You for Your Opinion, Doctor; We've Decided What's Best for Your Patient

The term *managed care* can stir heated debate. Many of my colleagues and customers communicated strong opinions on the impact of managed care to me over the years. The term refers to techniques employed to reduce the cost of health care delivery, manage utilization of services, and improve the quality of care.[14] Some managed care techniques include utilization reviews, establishing provider networks, and quality improvement programs. Types of managed care organizations include Health Maintenance Organizations (HMOs), Preferred-Provider Organizations (PPOs), and Integrated Delivery Networks (IDNs).

All of these organizations, systems, and techniques have two similar effects. First, they absolutely must control costs to remain profitable. Second, I've concluded that, in effect, they limit individual HCP therapeutic alternatives. I've drawn this conclusion from 17 years working with customers plodding through the mire of managed care techniques and organizations.

Cost control comes in many forms. Here is one example: You (as a patient) arrive at your HCP office. You have a history of Type 2 diabetes and higher-than-desired blood sugar levels for the last six months. Your current therapeutic regimen is not providing the desired outcomes. Your doctor decides a different medication may provide you greater benefit. Your physician has a litany of medications from which to choose. Will she prescribe the generic glyburide, the branded DPP IV inhibitor, or perhaps a new insulin? Or maybe you'll receive time-tested metformin, a branded combination product containing two medications in one oral pill, or perhaps a new biologic?

A notable and commonplace difference today is the controls a health plan (insurer/payer) exerts on the therapeutic options available to your doctor. These controls introduce several complexities she may encounter in the process of getting a particular therapy into the patient's hands.

One such control is the patient's out-of-pocket cost. If your pharmacist told you the bill for your 30-day medication supply will cost you $700, you might wince. Then you'd quickly assess the therapy's necessity. It's needed but the cost is prohibitive. You then smile nicely and ask what other options might be available. This brings to the forefront another tool payers levy to control therapy availability: the formulary.

The formulary defines options available to HCPs and the corresponding cost to patients. It may also identify different requirements to be met for a therapy to be approved for a particular patient. These include tools such as prior authorizations and step edits.

A consequence to HCPs of these formularies and their growing complexity is limited therapeutic options versus what they may want to prescribe and/or time and resources required to get a particular therapy for a patient. Before managed care techniques like these became commonplace, doctors would write a prescription and the patient would take it to the pharmacy and get it filled.

Today the patient may arrive at the pharmacy with a prescription only to be told her health insurer does not cover it. If she wants it, she'll have to pay the full cash price; this can be hundreds or thousands of dollars. The patient says she is not willing to pay that much and asks for an alternative. The doctor's office then receives a phone call from the pharmacy and, ultimately, the doctor prescribes a different therapy.

With thousands of health insurance plans available, what therapies are preferred, covered, or available to a given patient for a given diagnosis covered by one health plan? With widely varying co-pays, co-insurance, and/or deductibles that may apply? All this complexity adds work and requires more of the doctor's time. A direct consequence of this additional time (that the doctor must take to deal with formularies and managed care roadblocks) is less time available to meet with vendors.

Lost Incentives

Doctors, group practices, and almost any HCP in a health system were formerly the recipients of many incentives to meet with vendors. It was a rare office desk drawer not occupied by a pen or notepad dispensed by a biopharma manufacturer's representative.

I don't give pens, paper pads, or tissue boxes to anyone in health care and haven't for the last 14 years thanks to my employers' adherence to the PhRMA Guidelines. I view this as positive change—small steps on our journey to enhance our credibility and trustworthiness.

Back in 2000, when I was a new pharmaceutical representative for a relatively large company, my district manager was teaching me the basics. One memorable step in this process was the catalog review. This was followed by a review of my budget and how I was to best allocate these marketing dollars. We also covered laws like the federal Anti-Kickback Statute, the Federal Food, Drug, and Cosmetic Act, and the False Claims Act, which I was obliged to understand and adhere to.

Of all the initial training I received, I found the gift catalog intriguing along with the means to take physicians to sporting events, out for a round of golf, and perhaps some dinner or to simply provide them a nice new driver to complement their own golf clubs. All I had to do was submit rationale as to why Dr. X getting a new golf club from me would help my business.

My manager had limited funds for this form of gift giving, so he denied many requests. Nevertheless, some providers did get golf clubs and other items from us. We could take them out for a round of golf or take them to dinner, a show, a sporting event, or even a Neil Diamond concert. They didn't just get medical information from us—they enjoyed some nice entertainment, too. This gave them all the more reason to meet with us when we dropped in to their offices during their workday, albeit usually unannounced. Then most biopharma manufacturers decided to adhere to the PhRMA Guidelines published in 2002. That was the end of pens, golf, tickets to shows and sporting events—and another incentive HPCs had to meet with vendors.

"I don't have time today, Scott. Sorry, but I'm really busy." This statement started becoming commonplace in my territory and that was in the offices that weren't already closed off to vendors. However, we weren't dead. Reasons remained for health care providers to communicate with us.

Say Goodbye to Samples

Most physician offices had a space where representatives would compete for top billing—where we could see what was moving or not; a space that was sometimes overflowing. This space was the infamous sample closet.

The intent of samples was similar to the samples in the Costco aisles on Saturday: try the product and if it works for you, great! The HCP writes you a prescription and off you go to your pharmacy to have it filled. If the medication doesn't provide adequate outcomes or the patient cannot tolerate it, the HCP can recommend an alternative and perhaps even provide alternative samples. In actuality, samples often weren't dispensed to patients but were instead used by clinic staff.[15]

Samples also served another purpose. The Institute on Medicine as a Profession (IMAP) in a 2013 paper stated: "Ostensibly, samples can be used to benefit low-income patients who would otherwise struggle to afford a particular drug."[16] Some samples did go to patients who could not afford the medication. Notably, my grandfather, a wonderful human being, memorably stated another attribute of the sample process as perceived by the public: "Scott, you guys get 'em hooked on the expensive drugs by giving away free samples, and then we find out those pills are too expensive for us to afford." Ouch!

Regardless of intent, IMAP also stated, "Samples influence prescribing behavior: physicians who accept samples are more likely to deviate from current clinical recommendations when prescribing drugs, thus placing patients at risk. The vast majority of physicians report having accepted industry samples at some point in their careers.[17] Subsequent to these and other similar findings, some health systems implemented policies prohibiting acceptance of any and all samples by their institutions or their employees.[18] This has led to one more reason why health care providers now have little interest in meeting with most pharmaceutical vendors: no more free medications in the form of samples.

Would HCPs still meet with us? Fret not. Other incentives were still in play, right?

The Shrinking Speaker Pool

Many of the doctors we met with in years past were paid promotional speakers for one company or another or sometimes multiple companies. "Scott, I talk for many companies, usually 15 to 20 times per month, and my schedule fills up fast," one doctor told me many years ago. "So if you want me to talk for you, you'll have to get on my calendar quickly." That was my introduction to the real world of physicians who were also speakers for one or more companies. Some derived substantial income from these speaking opportunities, taking in hundreds of thousands of dollars over several years.*

One thing is for certain, based on research evaluating speakers in a representative's territory: if they speak for you, you are likely to see an increase in sales, especially if they speak in an intimate roundtable forum. According to a December 2001 slide presentation from Merck, physicians who attended this type of talk increased their use of Vioxx® by $717.53, whereas physicians who attended a meeting with only a salesperson increased their use by $165.87. With numbers like this, having any number of speakers in a territory appears potentially advantageous. The speaker also benefited: for every talk a doctor gave, he could be paid anywhere from $750-$2500.[19]

With so much evidence proclaiming biopharma industry influence on HCPs and how this may lead to inappropriate therapeutic

---

* Certain remuneration received and related ownership interests of physicians and teaching hospitals from drug and device manufacturers is now available for viewing at https://openpaymentsdata.cms.gov due to the Open Payments program enacted by the Patient Protection and Affordable Care Act of 2010.

choices, the speaking norms were apt to change and they have dramatically. Health care professionals are now obliged to very specific contracts and have set honoraria based on fair market value, not an arbitrary number set by the rep, district manager, or the speaker. Speakers are also often required to use a set slide deck provided by the company. In years past, there was also a perception that training speakers was only a means to further influence physicians with no real intention of having those speakers present to their peers.[20] All these factors led to a dramatic reduction in the number of speakers a company will train or contract with in a given year. So how might this impact a former speaker's willingness to meet with the biopharma representative? The impact is the same as that from all the changes presented thus far: the doctor may not perceive a benefit from meeting with you now.

Reimbursement Down + Expenses Up = Zero Time for Reps

Did I mention the doctor hasn't had a raise in years and has probably taken a few pay cuts over the last several years due to declining reimbursement rates paid by the Center for Medicare and Medicaid Services (CMS) and commercial payers? In 1997, Congress passed the Balanced Budget Act, which established the Sustainable Growth Rate (SGR) formula. This replaced the Medicare volume performance standard as the means to compensate physicians for treating patients covered by Medicare. It was a formula designed to align with changing health care costs as well as the economy. When costs of administering health care started outpacing the economy, the SGR formula called for cuts to physician reimbursement. Consequently, the doctor needs to see more patients today to generate revenue similar to prior years. The result of seeing 24 patients per day versus 18 is even less time for any activity not helping her achieve her objectives, whether clinical, business, or personal.

As if there aren't enough changes occupying more time of physicians today, the Patient Protection and Affordable Care Act (PPACA—commonly referred to simply as the ACA) was signed into law by President Obama on March 23, 2010. The ACA essentially mandated, through the use of financial incentives and penalties, the use of Electronic Medical Record systems (sometimes referred to as Electronic Health Records). These systems are costly to purchase and maintain. Upfront costs start at around $26,000 and cost per year starts at $4,000. The total cost can vary widely, but several studies show the cost to purchase and install an EMR can be $15,000 to $70,000 per provider.[21] Result: yet again, doctors need to see even more patients to pay for this system and the annual fees to maintain it. Wait! Aren't doctors already seeing more patients because of lower CMS reimbursement? They are. Makes you want to become a physician, doesn't it? Are you beginning to notice the emerging trend here?

Clinic for Sale—Cheap! Physicians Now Have a Boss

Finally, if those weren't enough reasons for physicians to prioritize their time with vendors differently than in years past, many physicians who were in private practice are now employees of health systems or group practices.

The ACA provided incentive for health systems to purchase solo and group practices. By doing so, the hospitals of those health systems purchased a steadier flow of inpatients. In addition, the CMS reimbursements for patients treated by a health system are higher than the reimbursements for the same patient treated in a solo- or group-practice clinic setting. In the Pacific Northwest, the private-practice clinic is almost gone and those private- or small-group practice clinics still operating are biding their time as the clock for EMR implementation expires. Those doctors get closer and closer to retiring, selling their practice, establishing a concierge clinic accepting only cash-paying patients, hoping the feds don't collect the fines for not implementing an EMR or just closing their doors and walking away. Among the American Academy of Family Practice membership, the share of solo practices dropped from 44% in 1986 to just 18% in 2008.[22] One family practice physician, Dr. Srokan in New York, can't even give his practice away—no takers. He says, "There's not going to be any of us left [in private practice]." Doctors are now employees. They have bosses telling them how to use their time.

Now, with so many HCPs working in health systems with one or more hospitals at their core, the rank-and-file doctors are no longer the decision or policy makers. Administrators call the shots and the HCPs oblige loyally. Controlling costs is a high priority for health systems; they have direct control over vendor access to their facilities and personnel and they exercise it.

Providing another hurdle, health systems often require credentialing of vendors to ensure we don't have tuberculosis, a variety of other contagious illnesses, and perhaps that we had our flu vaccination for the season. Health systems, especially academic and federal health systems, have restrictive policies in place regarding the work of vendors in their facilities, often prohibiting any contact with HCPs via email, phone, or physically by entering the facility without a pre-arranged appointment with a specific employee.

In short, the doctor who used to accept an industry-sponsored lunch for her staff while she spoke with the vendor for a few minutes is now an employee. She no longer makes the rules and is no longer permitted to accept lunch, coffee, or any other material good or remuneration from biopharma per system policy (lest it be reported via the Physician Payments Sunshine Act provision of the ACA for all the public and the HCP's leadership to view on the web at will).

Why *Would* an HCP Meet with a Rep?

So do HCPs in health systems, group practices, or the few remaining private practice clinics meet with any biopharma industry representatives? With such changes and evidence stacked against the prototypical pharma rep communicating with HCPs, why would a doctor or her leadership meet with a rep? If you think about what it would take for you, your spouse/partner, or a family member to meet with a vendor, the answer is likely of little surprise: it often depends on whether the representative has any resources relevant to the HCPs and how effectively the vendor communicates that information. And while some HCPs may have an interest in meeting with a biopharma vendor, they may choose to find the information or resources elsewhere so they are not perceived by their patients, colleagues, or leadership as being inappropriately influenced.

In my experience, if you're going to have any hope at all of communicating with an HCP, one simple rule is unmistakable: **you must have something the HCP wants or needs**. What you think may be of value can't be trivial or readily available somewhere else; it must be relevant, substantive, and genuinely helpful to your customer.

This begs the question from the doc, "How can you *really* help me?" I recently spoke with a colleague who reported that a physician customer asked during his first meeting with her, "So why am I meeting with you?"

What products do you represent and how do you support customers who use or might use those products? It's difficult to overstate how important this is to the success of a biopharma vendor representative. Meetings with personnel in The Everett Clinic or those like them are possible but only if you have resources they want or need badly enough—so badly the physician is willing in many cases to skirt policy or ask their leaders for an exception. These resources are predicated on the products you are working to support, the culture of your organization (truly "customer-focused"?), and your savviness. You have to know your customer's priorities and interests.

Are you selling the seventh ACE inhibitor, the fifth statin, or the third rapid-acting insulin to market? Is there substantial clinical differentiation of your product from others in the same therapeutic class? Are you priced competitively? If these are the pharmaceuticals or biologics you're attempting to advocate for and your customers are in one of the health systems in Boston, Seattle, Minneapolis/St. Paul, Milwaukee, or Portland, Oregon, you have an atypically difficult road ahead. Unless you have a territory with thousands of doctors in it, you may be exceedingly challenged for all the reasons outlined thus far and for other reasons to follow.

You need a product supported with resources your customers genuinely need if you're to have any hope of communicating with them to:

- ensure proper product use (appropriate patient selection considerations, dosage, administration, safety considerations, and other relevant product attributes),
- support appropriate reimbursement,
- provide updates on payer coverage for your product,
- relay safety-related post-marketing information around adverse events experienced by patients,
- disseminate patient education resources related to products, disease states, or other relevant subject areas,
- explain patient savings program availability, access, and updates, and
- provide appropriate connections to your company's medical and research personnel.

Without resources relevant to your customers, you have little hope of connecting with HCPs in these closed systems that now dominate more and more markets all across the country. The resources a manufacturer provides need to be genuinely valuable to their customers. Generate value and you have one key needed to unlock the door blocking entry to your customer.

3
The Prerequisites: Product and Culture

In this ever-changing society, the most powerful and enduring brands are built from the heart. They are real and sustainable. Their foundations are stronger because they are built with the strength of the human spirit, not an ad campaign. The companies that are lasting are those that are authentic.

—Howard Schultz, CEO, Starbucks[1]

Once you're in the biopharma field and you have some success, recruiters will begin contacting you announcing job openings with companies looking for talent in a particular area. Once in a while an email from a recruiter would catch my attention, perhaps because I was motivated to look for new opportunities or because a particular opportunity looked quite appealing in and of itself. When this occurred, I noted there were always two primary characteristics of a company or job opening that determined whether I would follow up with the recruiter: the product(s) I would work to develop and the culture of the company promoting it. Why these two attributes?

Because they are necessities of life in this industry—the air and water of biopharma vendors.

Access is already steadily declining. If your product is questionable, will the customer want to work with you? If the company culture promotes an unhealthy work environment, will it appropriately and necessarily support the field organization? Your product and company/business unit culture are key ingredients to your success.

A Valued Product

When it comes to human health and the products manufactured by the biopharma industry, the safety risks are potentially quite high. The health benefits to patients are also potentially significant. The particular products we support have tremendous impact on our potential to be successful in today's limited-access markets, staffed by discerning pharmacists, HCPs, administrators, and payers.

If your product is revolutionary but priced too high, payers may choose not to cover it. If your product is not clinically differentiated from the competition, is similarly priced, and the third to market, you'll likely experience significant challenges in developing business. If your product carries significant safety risks, has questionable efficacy, or is simply a different formulation of an already-available therapy with no clinical advantages over the other formulations, you may want to steer clear or perhaps investigate its merits in greater detail.

The product is at the center of your work. It's the foundation for all you will do as an employee for a given company. You are representing it when you talk with a physician who may inject it into a patient. You are that product to your customers. If you are not 100% convinced as to the value it provides, your customers will sense your apprehension.

You want to be sold on the value of your product *and* you want the medical community to believe in the value of your product. The days of open access where we can deliver marketing messages on "me-too" or "me-three" products are largely gone. Efficacy, safety, cost relative to competitors, remaining patent exclusivity—these are some important product attributes you want to research, assess, and understand prior to deciding on a company to work with.

The Company's Culture

If you're supporting a valued product, step one is checked. It's now time to assess the company culture. Equally important to representative success, even the potential for success, is the organizational environment spearheaded and implemented by its most senior leaders. What values are dear to the company and how are they supported by the most senior leaders all the way down to the lowest level of leadership: the district or area manager? Their leadership sets the tone for the entire field organization.

Specifically, how does the culture of an organization support the motivational, technical, and business needs of its field organization? I've experienced vast differences in culture from *collaboration* as a cultural norm to *audacity* as a core value. Some organizations say *teamwork* is a cultural value and then rank every member of every team, thus promoting an environment that can be seen as contradicting the stated value. One company had *integrity* listed as a value only to sign a Corporate Integrity Agreement with the Office of the Inspector General and subsequently enter into a hyper-vigilant compliance state for the ensuing five years.[2]

I've also seen *people* and *passion* published as corporate values, and tremendous training resources requiring copious manpower deployed in support of new employees. This organization reaped significant value by living this value in deed, not just word. Their representatives are valued for the highly-specialized clinical training and business-related support they provide to clients.

Evaluating and re-evaluating company culture is an absolute top priority for me as it usually sets the tone for the way an organization acts and applies its resources. You really need to dig into this area when assessing an organization because the published values may not always play out in day-to-day decisions and operations, and yet they may and hopefully do. You want to find recent examples of a company's culture in action. Particularly relevant are values pertaining to representative motivation, a critical element of which is incentive compensation (IC) offered to the field force.

Motivating the Field Force–Culture in Action

As a representative, motivation to achieve is paramount. How a company sets out to motivate the field force can speak volumes as to how it applies its values.

MSAs around the country continue to evolve such that access to HCPs is decreasing and pressure on docs to see more patients and produce more and better results is increasing. The challenges and complexity payers levy on HCPs continue to mount, taking even more of the physicians' time. These market attributes, among others, serve to alter a representative's work significantly from years past. As such, motivating the field in the face of these mounting differences is a high priority for employers. The question is, how do they go about it? And how could they go about it to achieve optimal results?

This can vary greatly from region to region. I have seen high levels of satisfaction and motivation in some areas and high levels of frustration and discouragement in representatives in other areas year after year, particularly with those in outlier markets. These are the markets where access to HCPs is more limited or where payers restricting therapeutic choice inhibit HCPs ability to prescribe a particular therapy. For example, sustaining representative motivation year after year in states like Minnesota, Wisconsin, and Washington can be a real challenge for sales leaders when those representatives are being compared to the performance of colleagues in states like Texas, Georgia, Louisiana, and Florida.

Such consistent and definite differences in MSA characteristics can be challenging to accommodate. But so can high turnover, dismal motivation, and frustratingly low representative performance when compared to markets with better physician access or more open access for HCPs to branded therapies. So the cultures and values-related question for sales leaders remains: "How do I consistently motivate my entire field organization so each field member will feel he/she has a fair chance at top-tier success given the dramatic differences in market characteristics and the total U.S. health care landscape?"

I've seen glimpses of possible answers to this dilemma. One of the most noteworthy yet is offered by the studies of Dan Pink. Dan researches theories on human motivation and contingent motivators; that is, "for this work, you'll get this reward." He's learned these motivators work sometimes; however, for many tasks, not only do they not work, they can be harmful to motivation and achieving desired results. Pink cites numerous studies where monetary incentives can incentivize greater performance in tasks involving only mechanical skill or routine, simple tasks. He also refers to substantial data (51 studies) showing that offering pay-for-performance incentives "can result in negative impact on overall performance." You can find similar findings noted by others, including Malcolm Gladwell, accomplished author on the subject of success. He corroborates Dan Pink's theory well when he states: "Those three things—autonomy, complexity, and a connection between effort and reward—are, most people will agree, the three qualities that work has to have if it is to be satisfying."[4]

This poses an interesting question about **incentive compensation** systems (IC) often used in biopharma companies with field-based organizations. Most biopharma manufacturers employ "if-then" incentive systems. They reward field reps financially, based on volume growth, market share, or other volume-based metrics. "If you generate this much in sales, we'll pay you this much." And yet the work we must do to achieve these metrics has become extraordinarily complex.

So why do manufacturers employ similar incentive systems when 40+ years of evidence appears to question their effectiveness? I'll contend it's the same reason big pharma continued increasing representative volume and doctor calls, sometimes to the point of multiple reps from the same company promoting the same product to the same client. Some companies sent more than one rep to call on the same HCP every month, or every week. On occasion, multiple reps from the same company and promoting the same product would arrive at the same office on the same day! The festering problem with this approach was that this rep-to-doctor contact worked; it generated more prescriptions. But that was then.

Sadly, this kind of redundant rep-to-doctor contact provided yet another incentive for clinic leaders to close their doors to vendor representatives (if they hadn't already) that much sooner. The biopharma rep population grew constantly until it peaked in 2006 at around 102,000.[5] Still, no company was willing to pull the trigger and constrict field force deployment until Pfizer began restructuring in November, 2007 and laid off 2,200 U.S. salespeople.[6] Maybe this is due in part to fewer than 25% of visits to physicians actually resulting in face time with a physician.[7] Nonetheless, the downsizing trend was launched and the rep numbers began a steady decline until they reached approximately 63,000 by mid-2014.[8]

Beyond IC

According to Dan Pink's research, people performing complex tasks in their professional work need three things in particular to be genuinely motivated to consistently perform well; autonomy, mastery, and purpose.

Allow Autonomy: accommodate their need to direct their work.

Promote Mastery: support their desire to continuously improve to a very high level at work that genuinely matters.

Cultivate Purpose: honor their intrinsic desire to do work affecting the greater good—to work for "something larger than ourselves."[9]

A field force member wants to work with a company whose leaders listen to and apply the feedback of their representatives. They want to represent a company that upholds values supportive of autonomy, mastery, and purpose.

You will want to see consistent examples of this in any company for which you choose to work. My experience shows me those organizations valuing field input and consistently applying that input have less turnover, more motivated employees, and more clinically proficient and astute employees than organizations not adhering to healthy core values defining their culture. These are the companies that attract, maintain, and consistently develop highly effective talent.

Here are some questions to ask of your current organization or one that you may be evaluating as a potential employer:

- How does the company approach motivating its field organization?
- Does it solicit and act upon the feedback of its representatives?
- What adaptations have been made to the incentive compensation (IC) plan in the last two to three years? Why were the updates made? How are they perceived by the field force?

One company I'm familiar with worked for many years to dramatically modify its IC plan. Finally, after a senior leader change, significant and positive changes were approved. The enduring impact remains to be seen, but initial reaction by the field is very favorable. If this change continues to be aligned with the organization's values, promoting some autonomy, mastery, and purpose of work, there is potential for substantial business impact.

Most importantly, whatever IC system a company chooses, I contend two critical attributes are required for consistent field force effectiveness: 1) companies need to ensure that autonomy, mastery, and purpose are integrated into the motivational framework of the field organization, and 2) sales leaders need to assess and amend their incentive plans annually to adapt to rapidly changing market characteristics. If a company consistently applies these strategies I suspect the field organization will be motivated to perform appropriately and honorably with integrity and sustained enthusiasm for its work, and the business results will ensue.

When the product and culture "boxes" are checked, it's time to continue in your research. Who are your customers? What influences their therapeutic decisions? How will the resources and products of your company be viewed by customers in your territory as well as their leaders? What's the potential for success of a best-in-class representative in your market? Are you selling a Ferrari to Mother Teresa or water to a man dying of thirst? Understanding your market's critical attributes is another prerequisite for success.

4
Understanding Your Market Dynamics

Thus it is that in war the victorious strategist only seeks battle after the victory has been won, whereas he who is destined to defeat first fights and afterwards looks for victory.

—Sun Tzu[1]

Many of my favorite professional conversations over the years have been with industry colleagues from around the country, most notably with colleagues working in markets other than mine. Learning the market dynamics of other territories and districts provided me valuable perspective on many key business drivers. How did people do it? How did some people win awards year after year while others languished consistently in the middle or bottom of the ranks?

In these conversations, I sometimes encountered savvy, professional, dedicated colleagues who planned intricately and deftly executed those plans only to achieve mediocrity at best, year after year after frustrating year.

I asked the district-manager award winners, who consistently won business development (sales) awards, how they did it. With one company, I found all these winners were in the state of Texas. I found this curious; the best reps and managers in the country perennially just *happened* to be in the state of Texas? This defied most statistical laws of probability. But there they were—consistently the absolute best in the country. One question lingered for me and many others around the country: Why were the Texans always at the top?

One contributing factor: unlike the Portland, Milwaukee, or Boston MSAs, in Texas and other southeastern states, HCPs still meet with biopharma vendors in numbers greater than other markets. Meeting with one more physician or nurse practitioner a day is more probable in Texas than in Minnesota where access to physicians is the lowest in the country.[2]

So how are representatives in more access-restricted markets to compete with representatives in Texas, Louisiana, Florida, or New York? You need to know how to assess your MSA and adjust your strategies accordingly. Every subject in this chapter can guide a professional in the due diligence process. It also provides a framework for detailed analysis when a new role is to begin.

Thoroughly assessing a new business opportunity or the current business is a prerequisite to accepting a new role with an organization or to executing a business plan. Due diligence can help ensure alignment between an individual's skills and the company's culture. Importantly, it can also provide you the necessary intelligence required to plan your business development effectively. If all goes well, your due diligence can establish the foundation of a productive, mutually beneficial working relationship between you and your customers.

Much of this information-gathering process is about defining the general potential of your territory to be successful, as compared to other territories around the country. Knowing the limitations and opportunities of an MSA lays the bedrock for the work you'll do to build business.

What critical attributes define your specific MSA? Here are some areas you'll want to consider and assess early in your tenure.

Types of Accounts

The first thing to assess is what type of accounts are in your MSA and what level of influence each one has. Following are some types of accounts that may be in your area:

Large, medium, and small health systems (groups comprised of one or more hospitals, outpatient clinics, lab services, imaging, or other services) – Larger health systems are becoming the norm as the pace of hospital mergers and acquisitions has increased substantially. In the early 2000s, the number per year hovered around 50 to 60.[3] By 2012, it had screamed to a high of 105 and then, after a brief decline in 2013, surged again. As of August 31, 2015 there were 71 health system M&As, setting a blistering pace similar to that of 2012.[4] As these systems grow in size, they tend to work less with the biopharma industry and rely more on their own product research and funding of continuing education. This can inhibit the dialog between biopharma vendors and these large systems.

Group practices (outpatient physician groups/practices) – These are clinical machines, churning out hundreds or even thousands of patient encounters daily, often unencumbered by the research objectives and priorities of academic health systems. Leaders in particular therapeutic areas may work in a group like this. These groups may have policies in place restricting vendor interaction with employees.

Private practice physicians – Do any remain in your MSA? Those that do won't be around for long. Expect them to retire, sell, or just walk away from their practices. Recall the primary care doc from New York mentioned earlier who couldn't even give his practice away.[5]

During my prior work as a district manager, the territories with the most private practice providers (usually more rural areas) consistently generated above-average results. The few remaining private practices also comprised the majority of HCPs my representatives could reasonably expect to meet with at least once a month. MSAs with more HCPs willing to meet with us are likely to generate greater success.

Academic medical centers (AMCs) – These include centers such as Oregon Health and Science University and the University of Minnesota Medical School. AMCs typically provide medical leadership in the area they serve. Clinical practitioners and medical researchers comprise the backbone of these institutions. They produce research in many areas of study and seek to publish this research in scientific journals. They also often employ area thought leaders (experts).

Military and veteran's affairs – These health systems/hospitals may provide medical training to students, residents, and/or fellows in particular specialties. As such, they may also provide medical leadership in certain therapeutic areas.

Skilled nursing facilities (SNF), long-term care (LTC) facilities, specialty hospitals, outpatient surgery centers, urgent care clinics, and others – These facilities may employ professionals of interest to your business development depending on the products you support.

Managed Care Providers

You will also want to know the impact of managed care in your market. How many insurers (payers) provide health care coverage for the MSA residents? What percentage of patients is covered by the top three, five, ten, or twenty plans? Does one payer dominate a particular area of town?

During a company meeting attended by every district manager in the country, I was speaking with a colleague whose representatives primarily worked in Alabama. He was generating particularly strong results compared to our fellow managers, so I had to learn how he was doing it.

I asked him about the payers (insurers) in his MSA. How many existed? What was the status of our product on the formularies of those payers (insurers)?

In some MSAs, there are hundreds of payers, plans, and systems, each with its own formulary, step edits, and/or other means of restricting HCP prescribing options. My friend and colleague in Alabama said there were three primary payers in his MSAs. Our primary product was readily available on two of the three. In other words, a majority of the HCPs in his MSAs could prescribe our product and patients there could get it for a nominal copay.

Payers in other MSAs were not as liberal in approving our product placing it on lower formulary tiers or not placing it on their formulary at all. The result? Much higher out-of-pocket cost to patients and consequent fewer prescriptions for the same product.

Understanding the payers in your market is a cornerstone to effective business planning and execution. Consider these questions:

- Can physicians purchase or prescribe your product without a prior authorization (PA) for the majority of his/her appropriate patients?
- If a PA is required, do your offices, clinics, and systems have efficient and effective processes in place to process those PAs? Do the HCPs know what they must document?
- Does your employer provide your customers and you with sufficient reimbursement support to facilitate efficient and effective PA processing in the clinic?
- Is the volume of payers requiring a PA for a product commensurate with the other MSAs in the country? Significantly higher? Significantly lower?

Knowing this information will help you: a) evaluate your potential effectiveness in developing business compared to your peers and b) provide you substance and data when asking your leaders for resources necessary to develop business effectively in your markets.

Peer Instructors / Speakers

One resource you'll want to pay close attention to is any HCPs in your MSA who are trained peer instructors, commonly referred to as speakers. Many biopharma companies train and certify HCPs to train their peers on the therapies offered by the organization. If your MSA has multiple speakers readily available, you can find this reservoir of expertise helpful when working to provide instruction to HCPs in your markets. Conversely, not having them conveniently located in your MSA can inhibit or slow this training process, slowing your business development.

There was perhaps some noteworthy excess by biopharma manufacturers in years past when it came to speakers. This excess, coupled with the Open Payments "Sunshine" Act spotlighting payments to physicians and academic health systems and the increased prevalence of policies restricting physicians at teaching institutions from speaking for industry, has contributed to a decline in expert physician speakers for all the companies with which I've worked (and for many other companies in the industry).

If you have any speakers, you'll want to work with them effectively and wisely. This subject is almost worthy of its own book, given the diversity of speaker employers, clinical skills, expertise, communication skills, and experience. For now, know who they are, talk with them, and listen to them.

National and International Experts

Few variables may be more important to your success than knowing who the national and international experts are in your territory. These are the clinicians and/or researchers who help define and set standards, and coauthor clinical practice guidelines and protocols. These are the ones their peers, legislators, and lawyers seek for expert opinion. Here are some questions to ask:

- Who are the experts in your MSA? If you have any, are they affiliated with large, powerful, academic systems or another significant leading system or group?
- How influential are they in the local, national, and/or international communities of their specialty?
- What research did they publish in the last year or the last five to ten years?
- Are any of them contracted with your company to teach local HCPs about your therapies and/or devices?
- Are any of them conducting research for your company or for a competitor? If they are, what are they investigating?
- What are their priorities, interests, and needs?
- What resources do you have to help them achieve their objectives?
- How long have they prescribed your therapy? What is their opinion of the therapy you represent?
- What impact do their employers' policies have on how you can communicate and work with the experts?
- Can you get an initial meeting with them?
- Can you get follow-on meetings with them and provide them consistent and genuine value?
- Do you have multiple HCP experts? If so, do they compete against each other or do they respect and support each other? Understanding how to navigate the seas of conflict between customers can help you work effectively with all parties.

Researching and uncovering this information can be of great help in building your business within your MSA.

Policies Regarding Samples

If your company provides samples, discover whether the customers in your MSA can accept those samples. The once ubiquitous sample closet is well on its way down the road to extinction. Fifteen years ago, my colleagues and I would dispense several cases of samples in a single week. Fourteen years later, none of my 16 accounts permit them any longer, most as a matter of policy. They have no sample closets.

Samples can be a very helpful resource to HCPs and patients when employed as they're intended to be. To this day, I present samples or trial product as a means for patients and their physicians to assess the efficacy and safety of a therapy prior to patients paying for it out of their own pockets. If you have customers effectively employing samples as they're intended, they can provide you a helpful vehicle to genuinely supporting customers' priorities and interests.

Knowing the policies of your customers around samples, trial programs, vouchers, and savings cards is a priority. Accounts that permit sampling are more likely to want or need those samples, and as such, have customers to whom you can provide a valuable service.

If they don't accept trial product as a matter of policy, know this: it's always helpful to present opportunities and resources to your customers. Policies can and do change. And exceptions can be made by appropriate personnel in your accounts. "No" today doesn't mean the answer will be "no" tomorrow. Always think how you can be a novel resource to your customers; the key word there being *resource*. Ensure you're clear on what value you are providing and how you're providing it. It must be relevant to the customer and delivered as the customer prefers.

Conferences or Meetings Where Your Customers Assemble

For a given market, a savvy vendor will study the organizations in that market and then identify any conferences or meetings those organizations may assemble. Thousands of medical meetings or conferences occur each year, giving you an opportunity to talk with customers. Perhaps you will join one or more of those organizations so you may subsequently attend their meetings and be privy to their rosters.

Following are three primary ways to identify these organizations and meetings:

Search the internet. Look for organizations comprised of and consequently defined by specialists (e.g., pediatricians, OB/GYNs, physiatrists, etc.), nurse practitioners, physician assistants, pharmacists, hospitalists, group practice HCPs, and so on. Search for groups in your city, metropolitan area, county, state, and region.

Talk to your customers, as organizations exist that are not publicly advertised (for example, local chapters of the Society of Hospital Medicine). There are somewhat exclusive local groups who limit vendor attendance to a select few approved individuals or organizations.

Contact the continuing education office if your health system or clinic group has one. Learn what meetings they organize each year and whether they like vendor support for those meetings. Some health systems still ask companies to exhibit at their conferences and occasionally to pay a fee to do so. This helps minimize or reduce expenses incurred by meeting attendees, thus potentially increasing the audience size for these meetings.

A systematic approach to this work is helpful: collect web sites and contact information, conference dates, groups soliciting exhibitors, etc. Once you find conferences that align with your business development priorities, get the requisite approvals from your employer and prepare appropriately to work the conference.

Offices or Groups That May Still Permit Food

Depending on the MSA, there are some offices or groups still permitting representatives to bring them food as a means to get time to communicate with clinic employees. You will want to identify them early in your tenure.

If you have accounts permitting this, recognize it's an opportunity to have meaningful dialog and truly provide genuine value to your customers. Recognize also they may not permit this forever. Clinics and group practices continue to be purchased by health systems. Those health systems frequently have policies restricting acceptance of anything from biopharma vendors, including food.

If you have customers who permit food gifts from you, ensure you are highly effective, supportive, and valuable to them. When a clinic inevitably closes its doors to the lunch-wielding masses, you don't want to be shut out, too. You need to be needed. For that to happen, you must provide definite, tangible, genuine value—not just food. Hopefully you have an employer providing resources of unquestioned value, as perceived by your customers.

Location Relative to Your Employer's Headquarters

You will also want to look at where your MSA is and where your company's headquarters are. Why would this possibly be important? It turns out data exist that demonstrate how advantageous it is for biopharma representatives to work in close proximity to their company HQ. This results from significantly higher payments to physicians who work in close proximity to biopharma manufacturer headquarters. This then results in a preference for the medications of that company versus other branded or generic therapies.[6]

The same paper goes on to show states identified as more corrupt (e.g., Louisiana and Mississippi) versus those least corrupt (e.g., Oregon and Minnesota), as characterized by data on convictions of federal corruption-related crime. These states have physicians more likely to receive payments from pharmaceutical companies and are thus more likely to prefer the therapies of that company.[7]

As if that weren't enough impact variance among territories, prescription prevalence of branded versus generic therapies also varies by state. If you're working in Texas or Alaska, things are looking better for you. Are you working in Washington or Idaho? You'll have more work to do to develop business equal to or better than your colleagues in many states.[8]

Customer Concentration

One final detail for you to properly assess: What is the concentration of customers in your geography? Are you working downtown Los Angeles or Montana's "big sky" country with an occasional detour into Wyoming? If you're competing against colleagues with 100 customers in a 10-square mile area while you're driving thousands of miles per month to meet with your customers, you may find your time on the airline or racking up the highway miles constraining to your available time for developing business, particularly as compared to your peers.

A Final Word

Gathering the requisite data can feel burdensome if you're not organized in your approach. Use a template or spreadsheet to document this information, as well as to track and monitor its utility over time.

You can stay abreast of new, relevant information regarding your customers and accounts through Google alerts. (If you haven't heard of them, Google them!) These alerts will email you when they find something new pertaining to parameters you specified. You can set them for a variety of topics, so play with them and find what's most relevant for you.

I've learned information about my accounts before my customers heard the news, thanks to Google alerts. Knowing the hot press on your customers contributes directly to your credibility and business acumen. Building those contributes directly to building trust with your customers, a fundamental tenet of your successful work.

If you're methodical, a detailed picture of the defining territory attributes will emerge, providing you a sturdy architecture to align your resources with the priorities, interests, and needs of your customers. Then you may begin building trust, earning credibility, and providing definite value.

Even though access to HCPs is increasingly limited, know this: *If* you have a product that provides genuine therapeutic value to patients, you have potential value to provide HCPs and leaders in your health care markets. If you do not believe your product provides genuine therapeutic value to patients in your market, you may want to make a change in your current work situation. For our purposes, we'll assume you sincerely believe in the value of your product.

Success begins with what you know and the strategies you formulate based on that knowledge. Product and disease-state knowledge are obvious prerequisites for success, and companies often provide in-depth training in these areas. Yet a critical differentiating skill of successful representatives and account managers may not be regularly taught by home office training departments because the level required for successful work is so variable depending on the product and each individual MSA in which it's offered. This skill falls in the "business acumen" bucket—how well you know the health care market in which you operate.

5

The People Who Make or Break You

When we seek for connection, we restore the world to wholeness. Our seemingly separate lives become meaningful as we discover how truly necessary we are to each other.

—Margaret J. Wheatley

Fifteen years ago, the recipe for success as a biopharma representative was as follows: "Go visit the right doctors, the right number of times, and deliver the right message and you'll be successful." This mantra of old, I suspect most would agree, is a gross oversimplification of what is actually required to generate success today in some markets. The idea of the "right doctor" is now far too narrow in scope.

Often, our challenge is identifying who the "right" customer is and then connecting with him or her. The one resource most impacting your success is the people who can help you and whom you can help. This includes three groups:

1. the customers who will most benefit from optimal use of your product or service,
2. people in your company who have access to resources and information your customers want, and
3. people in the broader health care community who might be able to help you and your customers.

These three groups comprise the human network for successful medical account managers and representatives.

Your Customers

As we identify customers, let's begin at the obvious starting line: your company-provided customer list. The list will, in all likelihood, not be completely accurate in terms of who is (or isn't) on it or who is on it and shouldn't be (moved, deceased, retired, etc.). You will have to do your homework and start researching the HCPs in your MSA or territory. Doing this work takes time, patience, focus, and endurance. Following are some strategies that may help you build a list of customers who are interested in employing your therapy, who welcome your support, and who have a vested interest in achieving optimal patient outcomes when using your therapy.

First, you must understand the requirements your company levies on you. Employers often do significant work to identify the appropriate audience for a given therapy. They tell you to meet with pulmonologists, neurologists, podiatrists, dentists, oral and maxillofacial surgeons, or whatever relevant generalist or specialist they determined has use for your therapy. They may also tell you to meet with pharmacists in certain settings (e.g., retail, specialty pharmacy, closed-provider pharmacies, or health system pharmacies). The company will likely point you in the right direction. Then it's up to you, the field representative, to start your research.

To find additional customers, there are many categories you can consider:

Generalists and specialists. Start with the internet and search for the internists, pediatricians, thoracic surgeons or whatever generalists or specialists are relevant to your therapeutic areas. Be methodical in your research and keep accurate, running lists. Identify whom you will want to contact and their contact information, a list for those you may want to contact, and even a list of those accounts/customers you vetted but may not be relevant (e.g., clinicians in children's hospitals will not be of interest if your therapy isn't indicated for pediatric use).

Nurse practitioners and physician assistants may have interest in your therapy. Your area may have local NP and PA organizations that organize annual conferences, so this is a smart audience to look into. Conduct this research on the web and talk to industry colleagues.

Pharmacy personnel can be quite relevant to your work. Consider these pharmacists: retail, clinical, inpatient, outpatient, pharmacoeconomists, infusion, pharmacy leadership, pharmacy residents, or students. Consider also pharmacy technicians, and others such as purchasers or procurement techs. Research your accounts online to learn what type of pharmacy personnel you have in your accounts along with contact information for relevant positions and personnel.

Other clinical personnel may have interest in your therapy. Examples include certified diabetes educators, social workers, physical or occupational therapists, respiratory therapists, ultrasound technicians, and many others. You need to know the relevant HCPs for your therapeutic area(s) of responsibility. Research your therapeutic area to learn what other clinical personnel may have interest in your therapy and then seek them out.

Registered nurses (RN), licensed practical nurses (LPN), and certified medical assistants (CMA) can be very helpful in building your network and connecting with other clinical customers and leaders.

Inpatient personnel. If your product has relevance in inpatient settings, seek out the unit managers, nurse educators, nurse managers, charge nurses, and nursing and physician leadership such as directors of nursing or the chief nursing officer. The chief medical officer may also have some use for your resources. Think, *How is my product relevant to this customer achieving her objectives?* Then align your resources to her priorities, interests, and needs, get a meeting (discussed in Chapter 7), seek to understand her interests and present appropriate resources to her.

Patient support groups are often assembled and/or supported by health care providers. As long as the groups permit you to attend and you don't use them for unabashed marketing, you may find them a helpful means to connect directly with patients as well as certain HCPs. Groups can be national, regional, local, or even specific to a health system or group practice. I often find them to be quite welcoming of certain resources I provide. Frequently, these resources are focused on disease-state education, product-focused educational resources, and saving patients money on their out-of-pocket costs associated with therapy.

Long-term care environments. This unique channel may be a key to future business growth if you're not already working in it. While resources are often finite for these frequently Medicaid or Medicare patients, the HCPs in this setting have some decision-making power, although it may be limited by insurers or the health system with which the facility is affiliated.

Personnel in your state government may have an interest in your product or service, how it's used, and how prevalent its use is by patients covered under the state Medicaid plans. Several years ago, it turned out that a few of the states my team was responsible for had personnel in their pharmacy divisions with interest in a business development idea I was researching and proposing for national implementation.

Academic health systems, Veterans Affairs (VA), and military health systems may also find value in your products and resources.

Division chiefs and department chairs. I connect with division chiefs as well as department chairs to offer suggestions and resources that may help them achieve their desired outcomes as they pertain to my product. They can also connect you with the most relevant personnel in their departments. When they do this for you, congratulations! You have unquestionably earned their trust and demonstrated you provide genuine value.

Resident and fellowship coordinators. Often, these non-clinical staff members can connect you to the residents and fellows who may have an interest in your products and resources.

Resident and fellowship program directors. The Accreditation Council for Graduate Medical Education (ACGME) has specified criteria that must be met by institutions it accredits. Program directors (PDs) are responsible for complying with ACGME requirements, which includes training residents and fellows. Perhaps your PDs will have interest in your products or services, and importantly, your knowledge and expertise in the disease state those products and services are indicated to treat. Be sensitive here, as the academic environment is commonly quite skeptical and averse to working with biopharma vendors. Dozens of papers are published detailing industry influence. Consequently, many medical leaders advise against even meeting with industry representatives. If you plan to be effective with this group, you will benefit significantly from sophisticated and astute preparation, and from being well-versed in a wide array of topics related to the therapeutic areas your products serve.

Continuing education personnel. The medical education department of your health systems is a required email, call, or meeting. They vary widely in their scope of work with vendors. Personnel in this office, often called Continuing Education (CE) or Continuing Medical Education (CME), may actually be excited to meet with you. They may assemble or coordinate grand rounds (medical lectures), journal clubs, tumor boards, or other medical education events. Certain events can get costly so CE offices or departments may request vendors either sponsor an element of the event (such as breakfast, dinner, or snacks) or pay to exhibit during the event. You may also be permitted to sit in on grand rounds or other educational events for your own education.

Others. Don't stop with the above list of potential customers. Depending on your product, there are likely other personnel who may benefit from your resources and expertise. Do your homework, talk to any HCP or customer you connect with early on in your business development to learn more about the array of personnel involved in treating those with the condition your product is indicated to treat. Learn who they are, get their contact information, and connect with them.

People in Your Company

The next category of people with whom you'll want to connect are within your own organization. During my time as a district manager focused on hospitals, I learned my employer was working with a national organization called the Society of Hospital Medicine. Upon researching this group online, a member of my district learned the organization had local chapters in some MSAs (including several in my district). This was exciting, as connecting with a local chapter could generate opportunities to provide customers with resources of interest.

The local account manager on my team did further research and leg work and connected with the lead physician for the local chapter. This allowed her to provide this physician valuable information and resources (personnel, information, material, and appropriate financial resources). She became one of only four vendors permitted to exhibit at the quarterly meetings of this unadvertised group. This opportunity all started from a conversation with our marketing group.

Your marketing colleagues are but one group of valuable personnel resources to you and your customers. Understanding the broader personnel resources your organization deploys in support of its therapies is a critical piece to solving your effectiveness puzzle.

Here are some personnel who might be helpful to your customers and, consequently, you (job titles may vary by company).

Marketing (professional or consumer). Talking with your marketing colleagues can be quite helpful. Had we not initiated the conversation with our marketing personnel, the local opportunity would have simply simmered silently in the background, unknown to us, waiting for a more savvy biopharma vendor to unearth it. Personnel in this department may be very well resourced with several groups supporting a brand (industry parlance for the product or therapy manufactured and supported), or they may be minimally-resourced and offer only a limited marketing effort.

These colleagues, often called product or brand managers/directors, may have specialized marketing backgrounds and experience, field sales experience, or both. They are often market research and field-input driven. As such, they assemble a refined data dashboard that provides direction for strategies to communicate the value of their therapies to consumers, HCPs, payers (federal, state and commercial), employers, and other decision-makers. Marketing leaders are likely to have responsibility for the brand P&L (profit and loss statement). This gives them responsibility over spending decisions. You may want to ask members of this team the following questions:

- What national organizations do we work with? (Learn this and then learn when their upcoming meetings are.)
- Do we exhibit at the national meeting of this organization? May I serve as an exhibitor during the next meeting? (These opportunities often go to the local representatives and account managers, but you never know until you ask.)
- What are our objectives with each relevant national organization?
- Who are the HCPs we're working with in this group and are any of them in my MSA? May I talk with them about their work with us relative to this organization?

Marketing managers and directors are colleagues with whom you absolutely want to connect, listen to, and provide with well-vetted input via the means your organization prefers.

Payer account managers. They typically work with large payers of health care including commercial, state and federal insurers, employers, and employer groups.

Group practice managers, health system managers, or other large/national account managers. Personnel in these roles work with larger medical groups, integrated delivery networks, and/or health systems ranging in size from local, one-hospital, or multi-clinic (seven to 10) systems to national health systems such as the Veterans Affairs health system, Tenet, Partners, Kaiser, and Catholic Health Initiative.

Trainers and training managers. These experts in your specialty are often excellent sources of information on a variety of subjects including, especially, all the resources the field representative or account manager will have available to work with. Trainers often exist as field-based experts working side-by-side with new hires. Some also work out of the home office and serve as national experts to train new hires, new leaders, and field-based trainers. They also provide recurring training as new indications, safety data, or new or revised tools and resources are provided to the field organization.

Reimbursement and access managers. This group specializes in helping health care providers readily acquire and get reimbursed for the products represented. Their work may include providing customers a list of insurers' requirements that must be met before a patient can receive your therapy. Their roles can vary widely, but they ultimately facilitate HCP access to the therapies you offer. With the ever-increasing obstacles to therapy access imposed by payers, the services this group provides customers can be quite valuable to them and, consequently, valuable to the health systems employing those HCPs.

Colleagues in other business units or representing other products/therapeutic areas within your company. Connecting with your colleagues may prove challenging, extremely beneficial, or both. The potential downside for your colleagues to help you is they may think they are enabling you to grow *your* network and subsequently increase *your* value to your (mutual) employer. Unfortunately, because many manufacturers in the industry reorganize/right-size/optimize their field force every 18 to 24 months and incentivize them based on volume-based metrics, it can sometimes create turf wars, land-grabbing, and fiefdom creation. These attitudes and behaviors are counterproductive to an environment of collaboration so sought after by sales and marketing leaders. I personally find that the more I proactively help my colleagues, the more they are willing to help me in a time of need. And those needs certainly do arise.

Medical liaisons. The medical, clinical, and scientific experts representing your therapeutic area work directly with customers and are tightly regulated by federal law and company policies. Often a prerequisite to be a medical liaison is earning an MD, DO, PharmD, or PhD degree. If a manufacturer is engaged in research, this is likely the group to meet with researchers around the country and the globe. They can answer unsolicited, off-label questions from customers and speak to published data not available to commercial personnel (e.g., representatives, account managers).

They are considered "non-promotional." They do not advocate or promote use of one therapy over another. They present data and relevant research, including the good, the bad, and the less-than-appealing. Their credibility depends on remaining adherent to academic rigors. Medical science liaisons also remain distinctly separate from commercial personnel. That is, they are limited in the information they can exchange, and there are often specific rules governing their meetings with customers and sharing information.

Senior and executive leaders. These are the ultimate decision-makers of your organization; they wield substantial power. When presented with a strong argument, they can move significant resources to support your work.

During my days as a hospital district manager, I came across a journal article detailing how a relatively small health system in Michigan researched and assembled a means to legally label inpatient medications so they could be taken along and used by patients who were being discharged from hospitals. Most hospitals interpreted the rules around this subject to indicate patients taking these meds home with them upon discharge was impermissible. The result was substantial waste and increased expense to patients, especially when you know the rates patients were paying for these medications.

My math at the time showed inpatient health care consumers could save more than $1B annually if just 50% of hospitals implemented this process. After reading the article, I spoke with the authors and learned their process was not proprietary, nor limited to use only by health systems in Michigan. I brought my findings to my leaders who ultimately directed me to present them to the marketing vice president. She saw the value in my proposal and assigned one of her directors to take my proposal and run with it. A national-level initiative was now being developed to discern how we might translate this idea into tangible and definite value for our hospital customers. The initiative was launched and now had the full support of the organization.

Not all leaders out there were so open—culture is very important. I authored several proposals for the leaders of another organization. They were centered on ideas and strategies to develop sales in what were consistently the lowest performing markets in the country. As my proposals were ignored, I began to understand the priority of accurately assessing company culture. The senior leaders wield tremendous power to make substantial cultural and resource allocation choices directly affecting the environment field representatives operate in. Talk to your senior leaders, listen to them, and—importantly—ask insightful questions of them.

Other customer-centric colleagues. Some companies are growing more savvy in their approach to developing appropriate business. Reimbursement and access manager positions appear to have been increasing notably in numbers over the last several years. Payers continue implementing copious control mechanisms (e.g., step edits, prior authorizations, tiered formularies, and closed formularies) to limit use of certain therapies. One company implemented a team specifically focused on helping health systems improve certain outcomes directly impacted by several therapies they manufactured. The team still exists as of the writing of this book. This is noteworthy because the team was not initially charged with developing business (e.g., sales volume). They genuinely worked to help the customer achieve their desired outcomes.

Another company assembled a team to work directly with employers to help them improve employee health outcomes impacted by their therapy. The thinking and case construction for these teams, I contend, is exactly the kind of thinking needed to substantially enhance future biopharma business development.

Pharmacoeconomic specialists/managers. I suspect this is another group that will continue to grow in influence and numbers. Pharmacoeconomists can articulate the actual dollars spent by a health system on a given therapy. They can subsequently compare this to what a system may spend on alternative therapies.

The term "cost" is frequently oversimplified when used. "How much does your product cost?" a physician may ask. It's a broad question—too broad. Cost to whom? The patient? The institution? The insurer? The employer?

Let's say their inquiry is: "How much does your product cost the patient?" That depends on whether the patient is insured. Is the insurance federal, state, commercial, or a combination of these? What company insures the patient? Does he have a deductible? Copay? Coinsurance? Is he using a manufacturer-sponsored savings program, if eligible? The complexity of "cost" needs to be simplified, narrowed, and focused to the specific customer with the interest or need. Pharmacoeconomists (and perhaps specialized account managers) are the professionals who can assist with this data analysis. Knowing this can help prepare you to optimally support the person in this position.

Clinical specialists. I've seen some companies employ clinical personnel (RNs, ARNPs, certified diabetes educators, PAs) to educate customers and patients on various attributes of their product, such as its operation, use, dosing, expectations for results, or troubleshooting devices.

Others. This list is not exhaustive. Look at your organization charts, ask your colleagues, and leaders whom you may want to speak with to help connect with customers. When you go to your corporate/home office, ask to meet with marketers, operations personnel, leaders, and others who appear interesting or possibly helpful. Be proactive in building your network inside your company. This will help you build your network outside the company as well.

Colleagues in Your Industry and the Broader Health Care Community

The final group of people to whom you should connect are those in the broader health care community. Fifteen years ago I met Karl, a friend and an account manager 10 years my industry senior. We helped each other with accounts and customers. We've each held several different positions since then. His work over the years included work in the federal channel, and he expectedly assembled a strong network in federal accounts within our MSA.

Fast forward to 2013 when I was assigned two federal accounts with access restrictions in place. He helped me connect to three key personnel and provided insight into the processes these installations employed to restrict access to vendors. His insight significantly expedited me establishing connections with customers inside these accounts. I aided him, too. Several years ago, when I was in a leadership role, I served as a reference for him and provided professional counsel.

As long as you're not conveying proprietary information, helping your industry colleagues (not necessarily your competitors) might be reciprocated one day when you most need the help. You might alert them to an upcoming conference or exhibit opportunity, or connect them with a local vendor representative association.

The Power Shifted—and So Must We

The days of visiting eight docs a day and delivering the right marketing messages are not merely numbered in many MSAs; they're long gone. As such, leveraging all available resources to help your customers achieve their desired outcomes is paramount to providing value, earning trust, and serving customer needs such that they respect what you say and do. Only then can you expect to develop appropriate business by aligning your resources with their priorities, interests, and needs.

Decisions are made and influenced by a much wider array of health care workers than in years past. And connecting with them requires a far more advanced skill set than in years past. Biopharma vendors need a culture supportive of the rapidly evolving health care environment such that every member of their field organization truly has a fair shot at achieving top-tier success. Senior leaders drive an organization's culture and this culture is key to how the field organization is supported.

The volume of people who impact a field member's success is substantial. The challenge is to know who these people are, learn what's important to them, and bring them genuine value. Representatives who track, manage, and develop their networks, while also building depth and consistently providing genuine value—these are the vendor representatives who are sought by customers and employers today. The genuine value (volume, breadth, and depth) of your professional network correlates intimately with your professional net worth.

Only two weeks ago, a customer of mine I'll call Dr. Lane was speaking with a colleague in a different health system in the area. Dr. Lane was telling her colleague how I had provided her some specific, specialized training that was particularly helpful to her. This prompted Dr. Lane's colleague to seek the same training from her representative, a local colleague of mine. This directly helped my colleague and her customer. This is network value—genuine network value. Understand, my connection with Dr. Lane didn't happen overnight. I had to contact her and earn her trust by providing consistent, genuine value as judged by her. This extensive process required several months. You can see, however, that being persistent and focused in your work can produce quite favorable results for not just you but also for your customers and their colleagues as well as the patients they all serve.

6
Achieving Your Goals for Customer Engagement

What you get by achieving your goals
is not as important as what you become
by achieving your goals.
—Henry David Thoreau

I learned a great deal from a bevy of strong leaders when I was in the military. One from the Air Force Officer Training School said of a group of candidates who were not working well together, "They're all velocity—no vector." What he meant was that they had the velocity to go somewhere fast but they had no direction (vector); they didn't know *where* to go or *how* they would get there.

When organizations and teams build objectives, strategies, and tactics, they provide for themselves the "vector" needed to achieve their goals. Often, it's the vice presidents and mid-level managers who define the goals and objectives for a group, business unit, or division. Then it's up to frontline managers and representatives to implement strategies and tactics to achieve those objectives.*

In the past, the most common objectives of sales and marketing groups emanated from a concept prevalent in biopharma promotion in the 1990s and early 2000s; "right message, right doctor, right frequency." This usually meant "See the highest priority physician customers the optimum number of times in a given period (week, month, quarter) and communicate the predetermined messages to them." These metrics were seemingly simple to track, and ample statistical evidence validated this method for achieving some business development goals.

As we've established, however, the climate has changed and so must we. With that in mind, let's look at what is meant by these three elements and then discuss the new goals we must set in today's changed environment to secure the customer engagement we want and need.

The Right Message

The "right message" referred to those key statements that would help the HCP understand the benefits of a product for an appropriate patient. Marketing departments did copious market research to define the marketing messages for a particular product or service:

- What words best describe the merits (and safety risks) of a therapy?
- What words describing product benefits produce the greatest impact on HCPs and are memorable?
- What order do key points need to be presented in to have the greatest impact?
- What key words matter most to doctors versus nurse

* You can apply the entire scheme (GOST – goals, objectives, strategies, and tactics) to your own business (territory or group of accounts). Companies vary in their approach here but I always find setting my own goals helps me focus my work based on the requirements and opportunities of my markets and customers.

practitioners or physician assistants?
- What messages resonate most with academic HCPs versus rural private practice docs?

Eventually, the "right messages" were defined and the field organization was charged with communicating them. The expectation was that providers would prescribe or purchase more of that particular product for appropriate patients because they had heard the "right message."

Today, the "right message" is still a priority for both vendors and customers. Vendors want to effectively communicate merits of their products and services. Likewise, customers want to understand the critical attributes of those products and services through as-succinct-as-possible language. Vendors need to discern how to communicate these messages most effectively to decision-makers and to leaders who influence those decisions. More and more, however, the primary obstacle isn't having an effective message for customers; it's getting the information to them.

The Right Doctor

In the past, the "right doctor" was the HCP with patients who might benefit from a particular product, particularly those HCPs with high relevant patient volume. Companies would provide representatives with a list of customers with whom to attempt a meeting.

Over time, some companies began to permit representative and/or manager input into the customer selection process. In MSAs such as Everett, Washington, my first market, this was a major change for the better, but it was often limited in scope. Only a small percentage of customers could be selected by the representative; the company still dictated most customers with whom we were obliged to meet.

After more time passed and access became even more restricted, some companies began permitting representatives to select all of their customers from a database of relevant customers in the MSA.

Again, this was a step in the right direction, but, where territories were too compressed, some representatives and managers still could not generate enough customers to provide the representative enough work or, more importantly, enough opportunity for success.

Another noteworthy difference today versus years past is that the physician prescriber is often no longer the sole decision-maker. That power is now largely in the hands of large payers: insurance companies, employers, and the federal government. If a doc wants to prescribe one medication instead of another "preferred" medication, the payer may require a prior authorization, have step edits in place, use quantity limits, or impose other restrictions limiting the doctor's options. In this case, the "right doctor" might not be a doctor at all.

In this new climate, the "right doctor" category needs to include every other position that might influence or make the critical decision in the broad process of getting a therapy to an appropriate patient. Today, this is better characterized as "appropriate customers." Given the diversity of customers in some therapeutic areas, this shift complicates the "right message" plan. As such, biopharma vendors need highly skilled, very professional, and adaptable representatives to bring genuine, definite, and consistent value to the myriad customers affecting decisions and appropriate therapy utilization.

The Right Frequency

Complementing the other two legs of this goal-achievement tripod, the "right frequency" defined how many times a company's representative needed to meet with a given HCP over a period of time (such as weekly, monthly, or quarterly). The doctors treating the highest number of appropriate patients were the ones to meet with once per week. Other HCPs were to be met with every other week or once per month. This was a common approach companies used to maximize business from a specific array of customers.

The prescribed level of frequency in years past, and still today, would also prove to be one of the many catalysts contributing to clinics closing their doors to vendors. Too many vendors were taking too much time from too many HCPs and staff members and providing too little genuine value. Then, as some clinics closed their doors, the remaining clinics found they had even more representatives coming to visit them. Representatives were still under expectations from their leaders to achieve the "right frequency" metric. This appeared to only increase the rate of clinics implementing "no access" policies. And all this was happening while mid- to large-size health systems were purchasing private and small group practices at a frenetic pace.

What is now the "right frequency?" Answering this question is complicated due to the variety of therapies, clinical and business personnel involved with each, cost controls, payer power, health system control, access limitations, and other factors. The optimum number of meetings a vendor representative has with a customer might best be determined by local managers.

The optimum number of meetings for my group is the number required to appropriately develop mutually beneficial business based on the product, market, MSA, customer employer (i.e., self, group practice, health system, military or VA clinic or system, etc.). Dropping in for the sake of achieving a "frequency" metric is simply not tolerated nor plausible with most health systems in many areas of the country. Just today, a medical assistant told me and another representative in my group that her employer, a growing health system with dozens of clinics and several hospitals, has a policy of no contact with vendor representatives due to the perception of favoritism possible with such meetings. If you don't genuinely help your customers, their policy is to not even communicate with you at all.

Perhaps today a more appropriate metric than "right frequency" for some biopharma professionals might be one focused on *substantive* business development. The desired outcome pursued by antiquated metrics is so highly variable that, even if we were to apply a complex and well-thought-out methodology or algorithm to derive an appropriate number of meetings, the number would likely still be quite arbitrary to the point of gross inaccuracy or irrelevance. A more effective metric might be a customer's measure of representative, manager, and company effectiveness. This topic is certainly worthy of more research and study.

Setting Realistic Goals

I once worked for a large textile service organization as a service manager of six direct reports. Our primary effectiveness metric was a quarterly Customer Satisfaction Index (CSI). Our performance on this index was a key determinant in performance reviews and merit-pay adjustments. A third-party vendor would call a random sample of our 800 customers every quarter and asked them a handful of questions. As the leader/manager, I needed to get a rating of a "4" or "5" on two key questions.

Similar to the "top box" scores desired by health care professionals on the Press Ganey and Consumer Assessment of Healthcare Providers and Systems (CAHPS™) surveys of today, the CSI provided us a basis for effective and consistent value-added work with our customers. It was also viewed companywide as the most accurate measure of our effectiveness. This metric randomly assessed customer opinion in every market in which we operated, every quarter. And it provided a metric we all trusted. Perhaps we didn't always like or agree with the results, but the sample size was adequate. So we trusted it and worked hard to do well by it. It was a robust indicator of whether or not we were meeting with our customers at the "right frequency."

Rightly or wrongly, the "right frequency" still governs the goals and objectives set for many reps. For example, the following objectives have all been required of me at various times in my career:

- Meet with at least seven to eight HCP customers per day.
- Spend your entire budget (on dinner events, lunches, coffee appointments, etc.).
- Meet with at least two pharmacy customers per day.
- Meet with at least 1.5 (on average) hospital customers per day.
- Dispense your entire sample allocation for the quarter/year.
- Plan and execute all your allocated training events for the trimester.

All of these "activity" objectives were designed to help the field force achieve their business development goals. The challenge, however, is achieving many of these "activity" objectives given the substantial diversity in provider access around the country. What if you work in a market where health systems have enticed most smaller, private practice HCPs to become employees of these systems? Those systems often don't permit samples, lunches, coffee, etc. Academic health systems may not permit their employees to speak for industry. Formerly common incentives to meet with representatives are gone but the "activity" metrics often remain.

So how will we do it—how can we achieve our growth goals given today's drastically different health care environment? Are representatives sacrificing genuine business development work to achieve "frequency" targets? Assuming our organizational culture and values are sound and the product we represent is valued and respected, we need to connect with people to achieve our goals. For that to happen, customers have to see we have genuine value to provide. Customers must trust us and we must be worthy of their trust. And we have to communicate in a way our customers prefer while being focused on mutually beneficial business development.

In short, our goals need to include **strategies to provide genuine, tangible value to the customers, as defined by the customers, via means to which they are receptive.**

Getting to Your Customer

In the previous chapter, we talked extensively about how to identify a new customer base. So how will we connect with those customers to get that first face-to-face meeting?

In the past, our customer lists were given to us. Today we need to discern who our customers really are. Who has an impact on the decisions health systems, payers, pharmacy benefit managers, and physicians make? In our ever-more-complicated health care system, quite a few people can influence those decisions. Our challenge is to find them and understand how they influence the decisions in their particular environment.

Consider this story. Our company had a new product that HCPs in the 16 outpatient clinics of a local health system might find useful. Those clinics did not permit vendor access, so I recommended my representative and I go to the top: the outpatient clinic medical director. (When casting a wider net for your customers, remember to go up the customer chain-of-command. If you really have genuine value to provide and you can effectively communicate that value, presenting this to a senior leader may provide you the catalyst necessary to connect your resources to an even broader customer audience.)

We met with this medical director twice. At the first meeting, we introduced ourselves, our products, and our services; then we met again to discern the most effective means of providing information on our new product to his clinics' medical directors. After we presented a few options, he decided the best course was for us to give him some product information booklets he would present to his staff at his next monthly meeting.

Understand, this man is responsible for hundreds of people, millions of dollars in annual revenue, and caring for tens of thousands of patients. A new product would face quite a challenge to pique his interest. But it wasn't the product that initially got him curious—it was all the resources we had to support providers and patients. The product was just one component of our service offerings.

We were nearing the conclusion of our meeting when I asked him if he met with many vendors. "No," he replied. "And, frankly, I'm surprised no one has ever asked me to do this." At that point, he'd been in his position for about eight years.

The "secret" methods I'd used to get a meeting with him? My network and email.

Securing a Face-to-Face Meeting

The word *email* conjures up nightmares for compliance managers, attorneys, and many of the rank and file. But given the HCPs' uber-dense schedules, proficiency and compliance with email communication is an absolute necessity for the biopharma vendor. It can be a very effective means of making initial connections.

That said, many major and minor factors will impact the utility of email to you. First, you'll need to understand the parameters around emailing customers. Get a feel for the norms and expectations in your company regarding compliant email. Companies approach this potential minefield differently, and there is always gray area in written policies, so it's wise to ask questions of those senior to you as well as your peers.

Some companies restrict email communication with customers to confirming logistics of a scheduled meeting. One health system in Washington State imposed a restrictive policy regarding all permissible vendor communications with their employees. In part, the policy mandated all biopharma-related information be sent to one specific email address. During my employment with one organization, I set about assembling an email with relevant new product information. It took over a year to get this one email message assembled and approved—that's one email, in one year. In at least one company, sending email to customers was vigorously discouraged.

Contrast this with one particular biopharma manufacturer when they expanded an indication of a widely-used product. In announcing this to the field, they included a pre-assembled email with all requisite details and helpful instructions for disseminating the message to customers. This organization viewed email as a required medium for communicating. (In the next chapter, I'll review effective techniques you might employ to fully leverage email communication to connect with your customers.)

Bottom line: you need to listen to and understand the priorities, interests, and needs of your customers. The health care environment our customers work in today is dramatically different from years past. Becoming very deliberate and attentive to the most minute details can mean the difference between winning the gold medal and going home in second, third, or even last place. With that in mind, let's dissect a bit more around "why" we must be more deliberate as well as "how" to do so.

7
Meetings versus Calls

They that will not apply new remedies
must expect new evils.
—Sir Francis Bacon

Renton, Washington is a Seattle suburb on the south end of Lake Washington. It's home to a major Boeing facility, thousands of families, some of the most agonizing traffic volume in all of Washington, and Valley Medical Center.

With the normal complement of outpatient clinics expected in a medium-sized health care system, at one point the Valley Medical Center campus housed a group of three specialists. Two of the three specialists were speakers for industry. All were involved in research funded by industry.

Incentives for these physicians to give representatives time with them were overt and generous back in the 1990s and early 2000s. Their sample closet was bursting with trial medications and savings cards. Caterers were intimately familiar with the office since the staff enjoyed regular lunchtime dining compliments of biopharma. It was not uncommon to find in the waiting room of this clinic not one rep waiting to "go back," but often two or three. While one rep was back by the sample closet, another might get a minute or two with a physician and a signature for their samples.

Representatives like me would drop in completely unannounced all day long (rep appointments to provide the office lunch and/or coffee were often scheduled). Never mind that the physicians were treating patients in clinic on a full schedule almost daily; we dropped in and expected some time. Some reps were even incentivized to prolong their time and conversations with the physician. Physicians and their medical assistants did not appreciate this. A result of this approach is perhaps obvious today.

Eight, ten, or twelve reps a day talking to physicians will take their time, especially when those reps are incentivized and encouraged to get even more time on every call (i.e., "Ask another question to keep them engaged"). It pains me even to write that, but it was not an uncommon tactic. That time with reps added up. Physicians would get behind schedule. Patients became agitated. And nurses were frequently frustrated when they were going home later than expected because the docs were behind.

So, not surprisingly, even this once-hospitable-to-reps office changed its ways. No more lunches with physicians attending unless it was for something they were specifically interested in (this was rare). Only reps with drugs for a specific disease state were even permitted to visit and dispense samples to the clinic (with no guarantee of any conversation with an HCP). And time with a physician was no longer available to *anyone* on a drop-in basis. By the mid-2000s, in order to see an HCP for any substantive period, you had to try and schedule a meeting. The time of drop-ins was done.

The New Normal

"Reps are just having a lot of difficulties getting into doctor's offices. About half the doctors, maybe two-thirds*, depending on certain specialties, are pushing back on unfettered access," says Pratap Khedkar, Managing Principal at ZS Associates. He understands well what representatives in some MSAs began experiencing 15 or more years ago. He and his colleague, Steve Bull, offered an alternative to representatives in a roundtable discussion: "Instead of making eight calls a day, we're going to take you down to six; and we want you to spend the rest of that time interacting with other folks in the office."[1]

It's fair to ask, "Why weren't these subjects being discussed 15 years ago?" They were. It was just not happening nationally because the wave of change was then forming in only a few MSAs. It hadn't yet developed nationally to the point at which the wave would come crashing down. With the national physician majority now largely inaccessible, I'd say the wave, a substantial one, is crashing. But the customers are still there. They didn't resign or disappear en masse. They are still accessible by a savvy biopharma leader with the product, company culture, and skills necessary to provide the patient-outcomes-focused results our customers desire.

Getting That Elusive First Meeting

If we are to favorably impact our customers today, it's optimal to meet with them face-to-face—a tall order perhaps, but one we can fill. Phone calls and email are options if needed. However, the most effective communication often occurs in person. It starts with the first meeting between you and your customer. You just need to get the meeting.

If you have substantive value to provide your customers, resources (including training they cannot readily get on their own), reimbursement support, process and quality-focused support, novel

* In some MSAs it is far more than two-thirds who aren't just "pushing back;" most "unfettered" access is terminated. It's "appointment-only" if they are even willing to meet at all.

ideas, and relevant data, you have hope! What you need is to focus on the broader application of these resources as a means to help patients receive appropriate treatment with your product. This is what will help you develop your business today.

Our objective is to execute mutually beneficial business development strategies that genuinely help our customers improve their clinical and business outcomes, not simply choose our therapy over a competitor's. This substantive work takes time. So what we need are meetings with our customers—scheduled meetings as opposed to the drop-in "calls" that characterized pharmaceutical sales in the past. These are meetings where the time is used well and both parties are prepared and focused on how the vendor can provide optimal value to the client.

The question for many of my industry colleagues is, "How do I get these meetings?"

With that in mind, let's review the factors we must first have dialed in. These are our have-to-haves; I call them "the Four Cs."

> *Customer:* Know whom you want to contact.
> *Contact:* Know the customer's email address, phone number, and/or physical location(s).
> *Cornerstones:* Know the foundational cornerstones upon which you will build your value and consequent relationship. What are the resources you offer with the greatest anticipated value to your customers?
> *Conversation:* Know what you want to say and present to the customer and why this information is relevant to her. If the information is minimally relevant to her, you will be, too.

In Chapter Five we reviewed many strategies for identifying customers and what their interests might be. **Step one, Customer—check.**

Step Two: Contact

Next, you need the contact information for your customers. This is where two critical skills enter the arena; your networking skills and your web searching skills.

A note on networking, especially if you're new to the industry: the first weeks and months of a representative new to biopharma can be quite difficult. Health care organizations and providers put up substantial barriers between us and them. Breaking through, demonstrating you're trustworthy, and providing genuine value can be time-consuming and laborious. It requires patience, persistence, and confidence that is likely to be frequently tested.

One notably absent benefit to the new vendor is an acquired network of industry colleagues and customers from which to draw (and eventually contribute) information and ideas. This is why network cultivation needs to be a critical development task for any new vendor representative. I recently assembled a list of former colleagues I talk with and can ask for help from at any time. They are spread among 25+ companies. I've called on many former colleagues over the years and many have called on me for assistance. I'm happy to see I'm not the only one who relies on a network like this. Today, I see much more often that my colleagues are no longer working as "kill-or-be-killed" vendors; they work with the mindset of "there's plenty for everybody so we help each other" (within policy and only where appropriate). Network cultivation is a valuable development task for any new vendor representative.

Another way to find contact information is the internet. I recommend you search the following for contact information:*

* Be attentive to limitations of use or other terms and conditions applicable to contact information you may find. Some references restrict use of the content to non-commercial purposes. Adhere to any restrictions or limitations on use in references you choose to employ.

- Health care system websites or other sites of a health care provider's employer
- Academic Medical Center (AMC) web sites (some local providers are affiliated with local AMC's)
- Individual provider sites (some will have their own side businesses and websites)
- Local organization websites (e.g., Nurse Practitioners of Oregon, Society of Hospital Medicine, local veterans groups, and local groups related to a specific disease state like diabetes, cystic fibrosis, or Parkinson's disease)
- The medical school websites where providers completed their residency or fellowship
- Federal Practitioner Directory
- Other sites—a quick web search of just the provider's name, credentials, and specialty may produce a helpful result.

You found their contact information? Good work. **Step two, Contact—check.**

Step Three: Cornerstones

Then, what are your customer's *expected* priorities, interests, and needs (PINs)? You could meet him, rattle off a list of 25 resources, and not have one color on that palette appeal to him. We need the best odds possible the first time we walk into his office. For this to happen, we need an accurate hypothesis as to what is important to him. Here is some homework to do prior to initiating contact:

- Where did he attend medical school? Complete his residency? Fellowship (if any)? Other training/fellowships?
- What is his specialty, if any? What are the recertification requirements for that specialty, if any?
- Was any of his training in the military?
- What does a web search of the customer pull up?

- What does his LinkedIn profile show you?
- What does his employer's web site say about him?
- What does a Google Scholar search reveal? Any publications to his credit?
- If employed by an academic medical center, does the corresponding medical school have a separate web site? What does it reveal to you?

All this research can be done in 10 to 15 minutes. Systematically gathering this information is helpful so you don't have to duplicate your efforts later. Spreadsheets, customer management software, or applications like Evernote™ are helpful tools for organizing customers' information. As always, ensure your notes and information are compliant with your employer's policies.

Once you know a bit about your customer, your work to align resources of interest begins. What do you have that can genuinely help her achieve her objectives? This is where knowing your resources intimately is particularly relevant.

For the academic physician, disease state and product-specific data and resources supporting research may be quite relevant. A department chair may have particular interest in processes to make her clinics more operationally efficient. A clinical nurse educator may find substantial value in your patient education resources. Billing, coding, and prior authorization focused staff members are likely to find value in reimbursement skills, materials, or specific knowledge regarding payer policies. Pharmacoeconomists may have interest in models showing how using your product may impact budgets whereas clinical pharmacists may find value in detailed pharmacokinetic and pharmacodynamic attributes of a therapy. Knowing the education and training completed, current scope of work, and even typical career path for the customers you intend to meet can help guide your offerings quite nicely.

The information you gather becomes the cornerstone for building genuine value specific to your customer. **Step three, Cornerstones—check.**

Step Four: Conversation

Cornerstones are now in place and you're ready to assemble "C" number four—your conversation. Focus on stating, in two or three sentences, your value proposition for this customer. This statement should be nicely refined through multiple edits and revisions before you write it into an email or dial a phone number. Hone the text until it is clear, robust, genuinely focused on customer interests (not yours), and—quite importantly—succinct.

You're now ready to focus on how to start the conversation. With several options available the question is, which option will work? For the HCPs and health care leaders of today, I recommend starting with email. She may not answer the phone nor be readily accessible in clinic or her office. However, she does in all likelihood read her email. **Step four, conversation: check. Get ready to get rolling.**

Effective Email Starts the Conversation

I introduced the utility of effective email practices in Chapter Six, and will describe here several suggestions for you to write effective emails to your customers with the intent of securing a customer-valued initial meeting. There are a number of major and minor factors that will impact the utility of email in your customer communication processes.

First, you'll need to understand the parameters your employer imparts around emailing customers. Get a feel for the norms and expectations in your company regarding compliant email. Companies approach this potential minefield differently—and there is always gray area in written policies—so it's wise to ask questions of those senior to you as well as your peers.

Then, decide which is more effective: a corporate mass-email to many customers or an email from you to one customer? ZS Associates reports a physician is six times more likely (5% vs. 30%) to open the email from a representative than a company-generated email.[2]* In this instance writing the message yourself is likely to be the most desirable method for achieving the outcome you seek: an initial meeting with your customer.

Your initial email to request a meeting with a customer is a critical event. Keep the following points in mind as you craft your emails:

Understand your customer. Research your customer as outlined previously. Then you can more precisely craft your email and begin to align your resources with the customer's anticipated priorities, interests, and needs. Put enough content into your message to give your customer some understanding of your value to her: the resources you offer that may help her achieve her objectives and goals.

Write with precision. Every word matters. Order of presentation matters. The salutation and close matter. The structure matters. It all matters. One word, an inappropriate greeting, improper grammar, or poor flow-of-thought can all result in rapid delivery of your email to the customer's "Deleted" folder or, worse, deleting all future messages. Be succinct; say only enough to communicate your intended point. Merriam-Webster defines "succinct" as "marked by compact, precise expression without wasted words."[3] Then read your email after you write it. Can you communicate the same points with fewer words? If so, you may consider refining your message. Be very intentional when you write, just as when you speak.

Use your customers' language. I once started an email to a physician with "Hi, Doc." It was presumptuous on my part to assume

* It is imperative representatives be intimately familiar with their company policies pertaining to email with customers prior to sending any email communication.

she would respond favorably to such a casual greeting. I wrote many emails that day and became complacent, almost nonchalant. Turns out, she was not a casual person in this regard. I've since refined my approach. Along the same lines, respect your elders. Doing so does not indicate inferiority; rather, this demonstrates maturity. When in doubt, be conservative in your writing. Always be respectful, just not overly so (e.g., "Dear Dr. Jordan, I know you're extremely busy as your CV is absolutely amazing. I've been trying to meet with you for the last five years—thank you so much for replying to me!"). If you're sending an email to a military doctor, they often go by "Dr. Taylor" versus the "Col. Taylor" they may use among their military peers. Email closings differ as well. "Very Respectfully" or "v/r" is commonly employed by personnel working on military installations. Also unique to health care is their language. My anatomy professor, many years ago, told her class we were about to learn a new language. We would understand the meaning of terms such as dura matter, transverse plane, temporomandibular joint, metacarpophalangeal and copious nomenclature previously unfamiliar to most. This became rudimentary language to our customers during their studies in medical school and several years of residency. Know their language; speak it and write it appropriately, and accurately. Your credibility depends on it and this credibility is part of the bedrock upon which any business will be developed.

Consider why the customer would want to reply or agree to meet with you. Asking for a meeting is the crux of the message. This is where you need to make some calculated assumptions as to the priorities, interests, and needs of the customer and then begin to align the resources you have that may be of interest to him or her. This portion needs to give the customer reasons to want to open his or her very heavy and rarely-ajar door to you. Keep this part of your message to no more than two to three sentences. Write it. Then reread it. Have a friend or relative read it and provide you feedback:

would your test reader reply to you or want to meet with you? Some customers reply to my initial message and want more information, then prefer to remain in email contact only. However, on many occasions an email generated a productive initial meeting.

Be professional but don't overdo it. They're physicians, highly educated and thoroughly trained but not omnipotent beings. If you put a doctor on a pedestal, you are then "below" her—inferior in some way. When it comes to your product and services, you are generally expected to be more the expert than the physician. When your septic system goes out or your water heater fails, do you call someone who knows less about them than you? No! You call an expert. For your company, you are the expert to most customers. It's your job to know your products and resources intimately. If you don't, you should not yet be working with customers. When you are the expert, trust and respect your resources and yourself. Don't belittle yourself by over-acknowledging the status or position of your customer.*

Focus on the customer, not yourself. Imagine you are Physician's Assistant Marie Kim reading through 20 emails during your lunch break. You come across an email from Doug Rep, a biopharma vendor who wants a meeting with you. "Dear Marie, I am your (insert drug name here) representative. I have many resources I want to present you. I have many years of experience and I'm quite aware of your policies. I'm available this Monday at 8:00 am. I know you're busy but I would really appreciate the opportunity to meet with you." Hmmm . . . It seems Doug wants a meeting with me only to help himself [you quickly hit "Delete"]. Doug should try this —

* You may encounter powerful, highly influential, and internationally-respected customers. I'm not implying we in any way ever minimize the training, experience, or skill of our customers. I speak to this subject because during my management years I observed many customers become uncomfortable when we were too laudatory of their position, achievements, etc. That being said, I have also, albeit rarely, observed the customer thirsty for our praise.

use the word, "you" more than you say, "I." For example, "Several resources we provide may be useful to you and your patients." Or, "I work with a few colleagues of yours in other institutions and they mentioned you may find some of my resources to be useful for your patients and employer." One more example: "My work is focused entirely around helping you and similar customers achieve optimal outcomes when employing (general or specific product name) with your appropriate patients."

Specify how much time might be required for the meeting. For initial meetings I usually specify 10 to 15 minutes, given the complexity and scope of my products and services. You may specify five to 10, or 20 to 30 minutes, depending on the scope and complexity of your offerings. I recommend a shorter time period for the initial meeting, since 10 to 15 minutes is more readily available to most customers as opposed to longer periods.

Specify a few dates and time periods you're available, making it easier for your customer to select an option suiting you both well.

Attend to the signature block. Write your name, any credentials (they matter in the professional environment), title, applicable phone numbers, and email address. Write all this information on one line with each section separated by a "|" (above the backslash on common keyboards). This permits your reader to see the information in your signature block without having to scroll down.

Make genuine impact. Don't oversell your offerings; if you do and you happen to get a meeting, you have already overpromised and under-delivered. This can slow or eliminate any hope of earning trust with the customer, a prerequisite for collaborative work and consequent effective business development.

Finally, proofread your email. Make sure you verify by proofreading, and adhere to all compliance-related policies, laws, and rules to which you must comply. Upon proofreading, if at any point in your message you question how the reader might interpret your words, you are wise to revise your text.

Example Emails and Additional Considerations

The following sample emails apply the points I just described. Note the differences in them.

> ***Sample 1***
>
> *Dear Dr. Jordan,*
> *I am really looking forward to meeting with you and discussing my products and how they might help your patients. Several of my resources may be of value to you, your staff, or your patients. I know you're super busy but perhaps we could meet sometime next week. Some of the materials I have are simply amazing! Please let me know. Thank you so much for your time.*
>
> ***Sample 2***
>
> *Dear Dr. Taylor,*
> *I am your liaison to (company name). The focus of my work is helping you achieve your objectives. (Vendor's employer) resources me very well to assist you with several training platforms, reimbursement support, and several additional resources you may find helpful. These include education resources as well as programs to provide your patients substantial savings on their therapy. I'm available this Thursday and Friday from 8:00 am to 12:30 pm for a brief, 10 to 15-minute meeting to review your interests and priorities as well as a few resources possibly of interest to you. Let me know what date/time works well for you.*
> *Kind regards, Scott*

What notable differences stood out to you? In the first example, you're communicating your enthusiasm (unnecessary), general information regarding your offerings (more detail is necessary), and general meeting guidance when specific guidance is more likely to generate a meeting. The second example provides relevant, value-adding content, customer-focused language, and specific meeting options making it easier for the provider to respond quickly to your message.

You may also consider providing even greater specificity as to your offerings depending on the customer's role in the clinic, group, or system. For example, a clinic manager is likely to be much more interested in resources you can provide to enhance quality of care, patient satisfaction, or efficiency tools and tactics to increase patient throughput while also improving outcomes.

Our specific offerings depend entirely on the products we represent. Are your products covered under Medicare Part B, Medicare Part D, by commercial insurers, or generally paid for by the patient entirely (cash-pay)? Is it injectable, intranasal, oral, transdermal, or administered by another route? Is it dispensed by a pharmacist or inserted/implanted/injected by a physician? These and other attributes will define the resources customers need to derive optimal outcomes from the products they receive and/or prescribe from manufacturers and distributors. These resources then become part of your value to your customers.

Follow-Up Email

If you do not receive a response within a few days, give your customer at least two weeks before you send another email. Timing is important. I tend to give a physician two to four weeks before I send another message. The customer could be on medical leave, family leave, or even on extended holiday. You don't want to badger her; you also don't want to appear inattentive or fleeting. If you really have genuine value to provide, your persistency is the only way the HCP and her patients will receive the benefit of your resources so stay the email course for a reasonable period. Continue to attempt other means of contact as well.

The second or third emails you send can generate the response you want. HCPs often receive dozens or even a hundred plus emails per day. Your message can easily get buried in their vast email sea, particularly if your customer is in a leadership role.

I've sent many follow-up emails to customers who didn't reply to my initial message. Sometimes they don't reply to the second or third messages either. Often times, however, they reply with statements like, "Thanks for your message, Scott. I'd be interested to learn more. Will you be in the area early next week?"

You may also present connecting via phone as an option for your customers when you send your introductory emails. Certainly the most valuable contact is face-to-face. Request this type of meeting first. So much more is communicated effectively in person vs. phone or email. However, she doesn't yet know you or know if you are trustworthy. She may prefer phone as an initial form of contact vs. face-to-face. Or she may prefer this as the only communication mode. Present enough value effectively and you'll likely open the door to a face-to-face meeting if it will help your customer get what she wants and, quite importantly, if you proved yourself trustworthy.

When face-to-face contact isn't happening and you have genuine value to provide, offer via email to "meet" on the phone. I tried this not long ago. I worked for over two years to connect with a customer in a very anti-industry health system, to no avail. I offered the phone call as an option to talk, along with a succinct review of resources I suspected may be of interest to her. She replied to the email, gave me her cell phone number, and asked me to call during the lunch hour one day to discuss my offerings. One step at a time...

The follow-up email is just as important as your initial email, if not more so, as the sun could be setting on the opportunity for you to connect via email. You want your email to stand out so make it relevant to her and craft it with the same precision as your initial message.

The First Reply

When you get a positive reply to your email message, you should take a minute to acknowledge your work—you did it! The first reply is momentous as it gives you a chance to do your real work of aligning your resources with the priorities, interests, and needs of your customers to help them achieve their desired outcomes.

You may also have quite a bit more information to work with. For example, if the customer replies with, "Dr. Jordan," that's how I'd address my next email to her. If she signs her message, "Cheers, Kristen," I would subsequently address her as Kristen. If she replies with just one or two lines, I know I should be succinct in future emails. Also, if she communicates interest in a particular resource or topic, I'll offer at least three dates and availability windows so she can select the best choice for her to briefly meet in person. Hopefully, the customer will reply with his or her preferred choice. When you receive this, clearly and concisely finalize the meeting date, time, location, and any additional relevant details (e.g., do you have access to the meeting location, do you require an escort, is a sponsor required to enter the military installation, etc.).

You may not always receive a positive reply as a first reply to your email. One very high-level academic physician replied to my initial email message offering relevant resources to him with, "NO assistance is needed." Roger that. Understood. So I continued emailing and eventually connected to everyone else in that department who might benefit from my resources. You also need to discern when to "cut bait" and move on or around.

Email Didn't Work; Now What?

If email ultimately proves ineffective in producing a meeting, move to the phone. Just pick it up and dial. Easy, right? Maybe. Let's review how the phone call might unfold and what we can do to get the outcome we want. The key—*prepare* for the likely eventualities.

When you dial the contact number for a customer, you need to be prepared for a variety of personnel who may or may not answer. If the desired customer answers, do you know why you are calling—what you want and what you need to say to get a face-to-face meeting with that person? If you don't, don't dial. If the customer answers, that may be the one and only chance you ever get to make that connection and prove your value. What if an administrative assistant answers? Or a receptionist? Or an operator? Or a scheduler? Or someone who doesn't identify herself? Or what if it goes to voicemail? Do you leave a message? What will you say? Play these scenarios out in your mind or role play them with a colleague. The imperative here is to be prepared.

A representative, reporting to me at the time, once called a chief resident with whom he was working to connect regarding a new device we offered. One day he decided to just pick up the phone and call her. To his surprise, she answered her phone. Not expecting her to pick up may have reduced his perceived priority of planning the call in greater detail. While the conversation was cordial, she never contacted him again nor replied to his contact attempts.*

When email and phone are ineffective, another option still exists, albeit to a far less extent than in years past. While working with one biopharma manufacturer, we made a significant change that would unquestionably benefit a large group of customers.** I set out to get meetings with the personnel in the relevant health systems to present the details and they could make their own decisions. Six of my seven customers eventually replied to my email inquiries for brief meetings to provide the relevant details, some after several messages. The seventh customer, the largest of the seven, would not reply to any emails. Phone calls weren't returned. Options were

* While perhaps seemingly disappointing to my representative and me, this event proved to be a very helpful and valuable training scenario for many years and is still being used as such today right before your eyes.

** Since the details of this specific offering are proprietary, I cannot disclose them here.

dwindling. This customer had restrictions limiting permitted vendor activities on their property. You couldn't be in the facility without a scheduled meeting. Alas, nothing to date had worked so it was time to take more risk, albeit a calculated risk. I decided to visit.

The information I was trying to provide was unquestionably valuable to them. Were I to be stopped in a hall by a staff member, I was prepared. Turns out, I got the chance to test my preparation. I walked into the pharmacy and was immediately met by questioning eyes and an inquiry from a senior manager.

"May I help you?" he asked, accompanied by the not-unexpected *why-are-you-here and you-are-interrupting-our-work* non-verbal signals.

With a courteous and professional *I'm-trying-to-help-you-help-yourselves* look, I replied: "Yes. Hello. My name is Scott and you purchase a fair amount of my product every year and as such, you get my services. We [have made a significant change] that could be helpful to your health system but no one here knows of it. Consequently, you aren't leveraging it for your benefit. I made a few attempts to communicate this to the relevant personnel, with no replies received."

I didn't get to say anything else. He continued looking me in the eye and said, "Wait right here."

Either he was going to get security to escort me out of the building (with subsequent consequences to me and my employer for violating policy), or he was actually going to get the appropriate point of contact. At this point, I'd worked for months to provide them this update. I had little to lose, so the risk was worth it and I was ready for whoever returned with him.

After a few minutes, he arrived with another gentleman and introduced him as the person with whom I needed to speak. "Scott, this is Richard; he can help you." Mission accomplished. If only I had done this several weeks ago, I might have saved myself significant time and energy wasted on follow-up emails and additional phone calls. Just walk in, ready to talk with anyone, clear on your objectives and, most importantly, very clear on what's in it for them to talk with you and connect you with the appropriate person.

That day, an email went from Richard to the chair of the Pharmacy and Therapeutics (P&T) Committee with the news I delivered. Impact achieved. At least the ball was now in their court and they had the information necessary to make an informed decision. Had I not worked to get this information to them, they may never have known what we did to assist them in improving a key metric of theirs.

The Parking Lot? No. But . . .

In no way do I or will I ever advocate you be so bold as to stalk customers in the parking lot as they arrive for or depart work. However, there is a very real chance you may encounter a customer for whom you have genuine value to provide as you work a conference, walk through a facility in route to a meeting, or even on an elevator. Much has been made of these chance encounters and the necessity of preparing for them. If you prepare for the phone calls you need to make, you are also prepared for the elevator encounter. You may only get one chance; what will you do with it?

As a hospital district manager, I had a savvy representative in Utah. I'll call him Randy. He was working to present an initiative that had the potential to help the hospital improve several high-priority outcomes they tracked regularly. He identified the physician leader to whom he needed to present the initiative and he knew exactly what he would say if he saw her. We had just attempted to meet with this specialist in her department and she was not available. She had also not returned his phone calls or email messages to date but Randy knew for certain she would have particular interest in our offerings. Ready to depart the floor, we stepped into an elevator and waited for the doors to close. Who stepped into the elevator just before the doors closed? Yep. She did. Randy recognized her, introduced himself, and told her very succinctly why he wanted to have a sit-down meeting with her. He was humble, sincere, and specific, looking her in the eye the entire time.

Before the elevator went down six floors, he was done and she agreed to meet with him. She was actually excited to speak with him and apologetic for not returning his messages after he said why he felt they should talk. He didn't sound scripted or rehearsed and the brief encounter was full of genuine value for her. The primary problem to that point was he just couldn't convey the relevant details of his offerings adequately in an email or over the phone; nothing substantive ever really is, as you lose the ever-so-precious nonverbal communication. The meeting happened shortly thereafter and a new business development venture was launched—all due to a few fortuitous seconds in an elevator with a skilled, mature, talented, and well-prepared representative.

Alternate Methods of Connecting with a Customer

This will happen: you'll send precisely crafted emails to HCPs over several weeks or even months and they will not reply. You will call. They won't answer. You'll show up and they'll be insulated from your contact attempts. Fret not. There are many alternative methods to make that initial connection to a customer. Here are several:

Referrals. Leverage your customer network; ask customers who respect and value your work to make an email introduction of you to another relevant customer you're trying to offer resources to. This works!

Meetings and events. Find the conferences, symposia, society meetings, disease state awareness events, CE events, and meetings of local, state, or regional provider groups. Connect with the administrative contacts for the organization and learn their interests regarding support from vendors. Do they permit displays or sponsorship of their meetings? If so, when is their next meeting? Who, if anyone, is on the agenda to speak at the meeting? Are any of the speakers your customers? This may be an excellent opportunity to connect with one or more customers when they're away from their clinic or hospital—likely a far better time to converse with them.

Non-standard forms of communication. In addition to face-to-face meetings, the value and impact of other communication forms, such as text messaging for example, should be recognized and respected. These alternative methods are rarely if ever acknowledged as a quantifiable and effective means to achieve goals, possibly due to the current limitations on collecting data. Be that as it may, I sometimes communicate (appropriately) matters of higher priority or urgency via text message, as some customers prefer this medium. Learn the preferred communication methods of your customers and align your communication methods accordingly.

Understand, Align, and Communicate Your Resources

The days of the traditional private practice doctors are numbered. So, too, are the days when vendor representatives can expect to saunter in unannounced to one of the remaining private practice physician offices and expect to get any time with a doctor whatsoever. "They (physicians) see themselves as a beleaguered group whose lives are made miserable by third-party payers, personal-injury attorneys, and hospital bureaucrats. Whatever idealism they may have had about the practice of medicine is being pushed aside by the concrete realities of hustling in the new medical marketplace."[4] We must work very deliberately and specifically if we are to connect with this "beleaguered" customer group.

Fortunately, opportunity still exists to help our customers help themselves and their patients with our products and services. Understand, align, and communicate your resources wisely and you can be effective in helping your customers achieve their desired outcomes while appropriately and effectively developing your business.

When our product and company culture are truly valued and supportive, connecting with our customers is mutually beneficial. Until this happens, we can do very little to help them optimize their experience with our resources that are sometimes quite helpful to the HCP, the patient, and/or the HCP's employer. Whether it's email, phone or in-person, once you secure your first meeting you need to become quite serious about preparing thoroughly for the encounter. Plan and execute it poorly and it will be your last meeting. Plan and execute well and you've earned your way to the next all-important step towards mutually beneficial business development.

8
Your First Meeting

It's the little details that are vital.
Little things make big things happen.

—John Wooden, known for methodically teaching his UCLA basketball teams to put on their socks and tie their shoes properly so as not to lose playing time.

It was October 30, 1935 at Wright Air Field in Dayton, Ohio. Boeing's Model 299 was on the field ready for the test flight. So, too, was a smaller competitor built by Douglas. The test was considered by most to be a formality, as the Model 299 had fared far better to date than the Douglas plane.

The expected winner, piloted by Major Ployer P. Hill—the Army Air Corps' Chief of Flight Testing—taxied into position for takeoff. Its four Pratt & Whitney R-1690 "Hornet" radial engines roared to full power hurling the gleaming craft down the runway and into the sky where, just 300 feet above the ground, it stalled. The plane promptly crashed in a fireball, killing two of the five on board, including Major Hill.

What brought the Model 299 down, especially with an expert pilot such as Major Hill at the controls? "Little things make big things happen," said legendary UCLA basketball coach, John Wooden, and he couldn't be more correct. Boeing had put a new locking mechanism on the elevator and rudder controls. Major Hill simply forgot to remove this mechanism resulting in the aircraft rolling and crashing shortly after takeoff— "pilot error." It was ultimately determined the plane was too complex for one person to fly.

The smaller Douglas aircraft won the competition but the Army Air Corps still purchased some Model 299s as test aircraft, since they believed in the plane's potential. The complexity problem, however, remained. How could they make this complicated yet very capable aircraft flyable? A group of test pilots decided on a simple solution: a pilot's checklist—a simple step-by-step list of all actions required for taxi, takeoff, and landing. The list made a complicated and intricate task elegantly simpler.

The Army ultimately ordered almost 13,000 B-17 "Flying Fortress" aircraft, as the 299 came to be known. After checklists were implemented, the pilots flew the 299 a total of 1.8 million miles. How many accidents occurred during this time? Zero.[1] That was the power of a simple checklist—a systematic procedure to be used every time the plane was flown.

Atul Gawande, a general surgeon at Brigham and Women's Hospital in Boston, Massachusetts, and Professor of Surgery at Harvard Medical School, writes of this story in his book, *The Checklist Manifesto*. He presents it as a compelling argument for checklists to be implemented into certain health care processes.[2] Thanks to my time in Air Force space and missile operations, I'm a checklist devotee. After reading his book, I quickly latched onto Dr. Gawande's suggestion. While biopharma hasn't yet found the checklist to be absolutely necessary, its relevance is certainly plausible given the potential for meetings with customers to "crash and burn" if we don't properly prepare for these meetings.

In preparation for our most recent national meeting, I read no less than 300 pages of study material, spending dozens of hours studying, practicing with anatomical models, and memorizing and understanding several important subjects. If I make an inaccurate statement to a customer and she consequently applies my direction causing a deleterious outcome in a patient the consequences could be severe for all involved. We need to get all the details right every time. That can be challenging, given the information volumes with which we must be intimately proficient. And simply knowing the information isn't enough; we must be able to effectively teach it to physicians—some of the most educated people on the planet. This is an entirely different standard versus just understanding the information. And that's the standard we must be at every single day.

On any given day, I'm expected to be proficient with the knowledge surrounding my products and services to a level where I can teach academic physicians* and their leaders, fellows, and residents how to safely and effectively administer my product. Each diagnosis manifests from different causes and is characterized by widely varying symptoms with copious treatment options available. I need to understand them all. I train physicians on five different procedures using intricate models to identify musculature, localization techniques, safety considerations, and optimal processes. I also support practices' reimbursement needs by understanding coding and billing processes to a point where I can offer solutions when challenges arise or when they don't even know they have an opportunity; I can help them find it. I support patient education needs, maintaining a

---

* Academic physicians, depending on their specialty, complete a four-year undergraduate education proceeded by anywhere from seven to eleven years of medical school and residency (on-the-job medical training). Some will also complete one to two-year fellowships after residency. From the time they graduate high school, physicians will have 11 to 17 years of schooling and medical training before they practice independently in their chosen specialty. Immaculate preparation is absolutely essential before we meet with them if we're really going to provide genuine value and develop our business appropriately.

database of web sites and contacts, as well as a supply of hardcopy materials and training models/resources for several indications.

One day perhaps biopharma manufacturers will find value in the formal checklist—perhaps a topic for future research. For every customer meeting, I seek to understand my customer, determine my objectives, resources required, priorities, and the myriad details associated with me being at and in that meeting. If I don't plan, I set myself up not only to waste the customer's time, but also (quite importantly) my own. Here's the checklist I employ—certainly no pre-flight checklist for a B-17, but routine use of this checklist can increase our odds of success:

Pre-Meeting Checklist (C.O.R.P.Y.)

- Customer – know what you can about your customer before you walk in (recall "Cornerstones" from Chapter Seven)
- Objectives to achieve (normally I type these on a laptop or tablet device)
- Resources to employ (materials, information, brochures, electronic/digital references, etc.)
- Prioritize (your meeting gets cut short by a page to your customer – what's the one thing you absolutely want to achieve? What's the second? And so on.)
- You (appearance, breath, pen, business cards, ID, vendor credentialing login information, passport or other required identification badges, etc.)

Planning helps us ensure we are sufficiently prepared. By planning for a meeting, we identify what self-study we must do, what verbiage we must refine, what background information we need to understand better and what resources we must refine proficiency with. Planning enables us to remember what we may have forgotten but need to know. Planning makes simple the otherwise complex.

"A goal without a plan is just a wish."
Antoine de Saint Exupery

Another Step of Many

The day will come when you schedule that first meeting with a customer. Congratulations! You applied the knowledge, ideas, and steps suggested in this book to effectively represent yourself and your value to your customer. And you communicated in a manner exuding positive, professional, and supportive intent.

This business demands plentiful patience and persistence. Success with one step means you just arrived at the next obstacle. Achieving your ultimate objective requires success at every step. Think like you're changing the oil in your car. The objective: have adequate, new oil and a new filter properly installed in your vehicle so your engine runs reliably and properly for several thousand miles to come. This seemingly straightforward objective requires many steps and much can go awry at any step, thus impeding or stopping progress. What if you misread the oil specs and put the wrong oil in the engine? What if your oil pan wasn't large enough to catch the oil without overflowing? Now you have oil on your garage floor—quite a mess indeed! And this is just an oil change—a somewhat routine procedure for any vehicle owner. Your first meeting with a customer won't be an oil change!

C - The Reason We Work – Serving Our <u>Customer</u>

You want to know as much as you can about your customer prior to engaging in the meeting as well as during your planning. This subject was already covered in detail.

O - Define Your <u>Objectives</u>

What do you want to achieve in this all-important first meeting? Every step in this process is important but maybe none more than this one: defining your objectives.

If a pilot flying from JFK to LAX sets a course that is off by only one degree, he'll miss his runway by 40 miles.[3] We need to know precisely where we want to finish or we're certain to be off course in short order, resulting in missing the "target." Once we know our objectives, we can specifically plan how we'll get to our destination.

By now, you completed a fair amount of research on your customers and the health systems, clinics, or environment in which they work. In addition, your employer has certainly prescribed some business objectives for you to achieve. If you have a healthy, positive, and supportive company culture, along with a product with substantial merit, you have a strong foundation on which to build. That type of company supports its field force with substantive resources that give you genuine value to provide. You have resources you can present to a customer and actually have her say, "This is very helpful; thank you, Stephan." And, most importantly, she means it!

Now we need to align all elements in this mixture. Your employer's interests, priorities, and needs must be at the forefront of this planning process; they pay your salary. What they don't know, and depend heavily on you to know, is how best to develop business in your market given local MSA dynamics. Variables such as managed care influence, health system prevalence, influential clinicians in the market, prevalent political culture (conservative, liberal or otherwise), legislative culture and relevant activity, and other variables all influence our ability to influence business development in our market. And those local market dynamics can have incredibly profound impact on potential business development.

For three years, a team I led endured the effects of legislation aimed at curtailing opioid prescribing by general practitioners (ESHB 2876, passed by the Washington State Legislature on June 10, 2010).[4] Washington was the first state in the nation to pass such legislation. A consequence of this legislation was hundreds of clinicians not specifically trained in pain management (and often their employers) decided they were no longer going to manage chronic pain patients or prescribe opioids of any significance. HCP willingness to prescribe opioid medications plummeted in Washington state. Managed care and any other organizations involved in the decision and delivery of these medications to patients also began to exert even more influence over formularies and available options, further limiting opioid prescribing. These factors, along with the rise of managed care and the prevalence of health systems (and the corresponding dearth of more-welcoming private practice HCPs) in the market made the market brutally difficult to succeed in compared to others across the country. In addition, prescribers and health system leaders interpreted the new rules quite differently. This set the stage for our challenge: The primary product we were marketing in this environment was novel, but still an opioid.*

Given our market conditions, our objectives with individual customers were quite different than those of many colleagues across the nation. We weren't just working to educate them on a new product. We were working to facilitate customer perception around the safety and effectiveness of our specific therapeutic class, support new state rule understanding by clinicians and leaders, and educate HCPs on the utility and managed care status of our product for prescribing to appropriate patients. Our task was formidable.

---

* Given the substantial and recent national attention on opioid abuse in the US, a Footnote is warranted here. Opioid prescribing in the United States is still grossly out of control. The US has less than 5% of the population on earth but we consume the majority (approximately 80%) of opioid drugs available on our planet. Mainstream media generalize opioids. We commonly hear about hydrocodone (with acetaminophen is called Vicodin™) and oxycodone (with acetaminophen is called Percocet™) products. But opioids like buprenorphine and methadone are effectively used to wean people physically dependent on opioids off them. There are several different prescription opioids available and they bind differently to different opioid receptors in the body. There are significant differences in the pharmacokinetics and pharmacodynamics of opioids and, as such, significant differences in their effects on the human body.

Our objectives for every customer meeting required the utmost refinement were we to have any hope of success.

You may recall a meeting I described earlier in this book between me, a representative from my team, and an outpatient clinic medical director for a large health system. We had two objectives for our meeting. The first was that my representative and I would understand the director's priorities, interests, and needs (PINs) related to treatment of patients with a specific condition. The second was that he would recognize the alignment of our product with his PINs and be willing to commit to communicating the relevant details to appropriate HCPs in his clinics.

These objectives were different than objectives we may set for a meeting with, say, a nurse practitioner in a small, rural group practice. She treats 20 or more patients per day at least five days per week. Many patients are quite complex and sometimes even belligerent to her. She already has some understanding of our product and most of her patients are insured by Medicaid. Objectives we might set for a meeting with a client like this would be that by the end of our meeting:

- the representative would understand the customer's priorities, interests, and needs related to treatment of patients with the relevant disease state,
- the clinician would understand the utility of our product for appropriate patients,
- the HCP would understand all critical safety and usage attributes of the product to the point that she could effectively communicate this information to patients,
- the HCP would understand Medicaid's requirements to get our medication covered to treat appropriate patients, and
- the clinician thinks of a specific patient she feels is appropriate for the therapy and is willing to prescribe it for him.

When defining objectives for a meeting, you must think from the perspective of the specific customer with whom you're meeting. Consider what information the HCP will require to choose your therapy for an appropriate patient as well as the critical elements in play to get your medication from the manufacturer or pharmacy to that patient. Then define your objectives accordingly. If I were Dr. Smith, why would I want to treat my patient with this product? What do I need to know to prescribe/administer it? What will be the out-of-pocket cost to my patient? What adverse events might my patient experience and how deleterious might they be? When should my patients expect some benefit from this medication? Is a prior authorization required? What conditions must be met before insurers will approve the medication?

The examples presented thus far are for HCPs who may decide to treat a patient with your therapy. But don't limit yourself to just this audience. If your product is appropriate for inpatient use, many more personnel may venture into the decision-making process. If HCPs who may choose your therapy are part of a health system, several additional parties may have interest in your product and/or the use of your product by their HCPs. The same thought process, however, most certainly applies: you must think from the perspective of the specific customer with whom you are meeting. What's important to a clinic business manager or charge nurse about your therapy? What does a clinical pharmacist or nurse education manager need to know about your therapy and to what level do they need to know or understand it? Will they need to counsel patients? Will they need to present it to the P & T Committee? Will they, or people who report to them, need to call a payer to get a prior authorization? See their world from their vantage point and then determine your meeting objectives.

R - Gather Your <u>Resources</u>

By now you should have some relevant information to help you understand what might be of greatest interest to this customer. Your objectives are defined and you're ready to gather the resources necessary for a successful meeting.*

You will need names/contact information, visual references, digital resources, training models, instructional workbooks, patient education booklets, training kits, links to video/online references, other hardcopy references, product monograph, and training resource references, and so on. If you don't have what you need, get it—preferably in plenty of time. Be resourceful. Ask colleagues. Place an order with your supply warehouse. Check your storage locker, your closet, and your garage. Contact your manager or someone in marketing who can provide resources on short notice. Validate and ensure currency of online references. Ensure contact information is current and accurate.

Then, once you collect all necessary references, make sure you are proficient in presenting them. If you give a customer a reference without explaining what's in it or its utility, it is quite likely to be forgotten or discarded in short order. Why might she want or value the resource? Why might her patient want or value the resource? Always present a resource or reference to a customer from her vantage point and how it might help her achieve her objectives or desired outcomes for her clinic, business, or health system and, most importantly, her patients.

A final note on resources:

- Have any materials you'll require prepared, handy, clean, organized, and up and running.
- Have a functioning pen handy for pointing and writing.
- Ensure any batteries (phone, computer, tablet) are more-than-adequately charged and the devices are functioning properly.
- Will you require Wi-Fi or cellular data during your meeting?

---

* Ensure all resources you plan to reference or provide to your customers are appropriate, compliant, approved or otherwise permitted by your employer.

Will it be available in your meeting place? Investigate availability before the meeting or devise a Plan B.

P - Prioritize Aggressively

If we fail to prioritize our objectives, we are still likely to achieve some outcomes. We may, however, not achieve the most advantageous outcomes. Consciously prioritizing helps ensure we make the most of the very precious time we will have with our customers.

Here's a simple strategy I use: If you can only discuss one item with your customer, identify what that item is. This is objective #1. If you can only discuss one more item with your customer, what would it be? This is objective #2. Continue through your list of objectives until they are all numbered. There's your list of prioritized objectives.

The first few times you complete this prioritization, it might seem as if every objective is an absolute necessity. This may feel true. However, imagine your customer receives an urgent call from her child's kindergarten teacher and has to abruptly cut your meeting short. You did not prioritize your objectives, so you're focusing on a lower priority item when the phone erupts with the meeting-termination siren. Unfortunately, your priorities are not certain, so the most important objectives will never be covered. You won't execute many meetings this way before you become a fervent advocate for prioritizing!

Another benefit: if you employ this strategy consistently, you'll become quite adept at it, enabling you to complete more high-value work faster.

Y - Trivial Details? No Such Thing – Attend to You

There is no detail too small to consider. Is what you plan to wear appropriate? What if you encounter traffic delays getting to your meeting? What if you don't have the hard copy resource you wanted to review with your customer? What if you had too many onions on your sandwich at lunch? Did a couple drops of your morning coffee get on your shirt? What if . . . ? *Oh no. What will I do?*

You have the meeting. Your objectives are defined. You are well-trained and thoroughly prepared to this point. Your customer is awaiting your arrival with only the 30 minutes she allocated to spare before her next patient will be roomed and ready. She hopes to get some useful information from you, as well as a couple of her questions answered. You get in your car to drive to her office and realize you are almost out of gas. Then you look down at your pants and see a nice coffee stain recently emerged. You check the traffic report and learn of an accident blocking the route you planned to take. The alternate route adds 20 to 30 minutes to your travel time. The last time you ate was 6:00 a.m. and now it's noon. Your previous appointment ran long and now you're really short on time. And you still need to check in at the vendor credentialing kiosk—will the printer have paper? Will it be functioning properly? *How could all of this go so wrong, all at the same time? What happened to the plan?!*

Consider these scenarios when deciding whether you ought to plan your meeting in fine detail: If you don't, the first meeting a customer affords you may be the last time you ever communicate with that customer. Skeptical or cynical customers may view your tardiness, unprofessional appearance, excuse for non-preparedness, or drowsy eyes due to lack of sleep as disinterest, having low standards, or inability to help her. Worse, she may feel you were dishonest or that you exaggerated the actual value/support you can provide. Investing time and attending to the details can reroute your meeting from crisis management to highly productive. Here are some details you may find helpful to integrate into your planning:

Your garments:

- Plan your wardrobe: dress commensurate with your customer without overdressing. Khakis/pants and lightweight hikers or boots are appropriate for the fall season in Montana. If your customer typically wears a suit jacket or business suit, the same rule applies.

- Check your clothing for dander or lint and ensure it's removed.
- Have a Plan B ready should you get a stain on your clothing (a Tide-to-Go ® stick, extra shirt, etc.)

Your hygiene:

- Attend to your personal hygiene the night before. No one wants to see the dirt under your fingernails from working in the yard as you're pointing to an item of interest to your customer. Ensure you and your hands are neat in appearance.
- Keep a toothbrush in your vehicle. Will your meeting take place after a lunch where you enjoyed a nice spinach salad, the remnants of which are prominently displayed between your front teeth?
- Have some gum or mints handy to assist you in healing malodorous breath.
- Leave yourself extra time. Running generates heat and heat generates sweat; sweat can generate an unpleasant aroma. Your unpleasant aroma doesn't increase a customer's interest in future meetings.
- Give yourself time to visit a restroom before your meeting. Aside from answering nature's call, you can clean your hands and inspect your pearly whites for cleanliness.

Getting to the meeting:

- Have more than enough fuel in your vehicle.
- Know the driving route you will take to her office/clinic and be familiar with alternate routes.
- Know how to get all the way to the exact meeting location. For example, is it an office deep within a large hospital? This is but one reason to allow yourself extra time in transit to your critical first meeting.

- Will parking be a challenge? Are you meeting at a large, academic medical center in a large MSA? Do you know where you will park? If you need to arrive even earlier to get a parking place or trek the half-mile from your parking place to your customer's office, do so. You might be glad you did.
- Be prepared for weather and road conditions. There is a mountain range between my home and many of my customers. These mountain passes can require traction tires or all-wheel drive vehicles, or they may be closed for a period. As needed, be prepared for adverse weather (hat, gloves, coat, ice scraper and chains in the car, vehicle properly maintained with adequate tires, charged battery, functioning wiper blades, etc.) Keep your vehicle well-maintained.
- Did I mention you will benefit from allowing yourself extra time to get to the meeting location . . . ?

A disclaimer is important here as curve balls may come at you despite your best efforts to cover all the bases. The objective of this chapter is to help you minimize avoidable obstacles and maximize your odds of achieving your desired outcomes from the critical first meeting.

Congratulations on Getting to "the Front Door"!

Your future business development through mutually beneficial customer support is largely dependent on what happens after you walk through that door and into your first in-person meeting. Earning a meeting like the one you are about to walk into is a major achievement and, as such, merits your proactive commitment to plan effectively.

Another benefit of meticulous planning is that it gives you a concrete foundation of confidence. In my experience, I was always most nervous when I was least prepared. I'm least nervous when I'm best prepared. Nerves and anxiety inhibit my ability to think clearly and quickly. And so it is that preparation calms my nerves and increases my effectiveness in achieving the desired outcomes.

If we work effectively enough to earn a meeting with a customer, we're certainly not going to leave the outcome to chance; we will plan. Far too much is at stake to gamble with our business, our customers, the health systems that employ them, and the patients we all ultimately serve.

Steven Covey, in his seminal work *The 7 Habits of Highly Effective People*, identified his second habit as, "Begin with the end in mind." This habit, he states, is "based on the principle that all things are created twice. There's a mental or first creation and a physical or second creation to all things."[5] When we plan well and wisely, we prepare ourselves to achieve our objectives — the second creation.

To help bring that second creation to life, we'll spend some time now on the single most important attribute of your dialog with customers: questions.

The quality of a leader cannot be judged by the answers he gives; but by the questions he asks.
Simon Sinek

9
Getting the Most from Your Meetings

A categorical imperative would be one which represented an action as objectively necessary in itself, without reference to any other purpose.
—Immanuel Kant

In 1980 at Lake Placid, New York, the United States Olympic men's hockey team, coached by Herb Brooks, bested the team from the Soviet Union in the game dubbed the "miracle on ice." For the Unites States, embroiled in a cold war with the Soviet Union and working through a recession, this win came at a time like no other. The gravity of this victory was beautifully characterized by the simple question commentator Al Michaels posed as the clock approached zero, "Do you believe in miracles?"

This was a monumental victory for the US, but it most certainly didn't manifest in just those 60 minutes on the ice that day in New York. This victory was won in the months preceding the game as the men worked, studied, practiced, learned, failed repeatedly, and got back up, over and over again. They continued working to build their skills into a harmonious symmetry of power, speed, accuracy, and finesse. They developed into a fluid team, anticipating each other's moves on the ice. Individually, each man developed his own vision, strength, endurance, accuracy, reaction time, and overall improved his skills to the point that on February 22, 1980, when it mattered most, they gave their very best, executed their plan, and achieved their objective.

They achieved it because they prepared. Coach Brooks planned; the team trained and executed the plan. And they did their absolute best. All their months of work culminated beautifully on that cold, beautiful day in February. And that's the moral of the story: we apply our skills and work deliberately, sometimes for many months, to prepare for that first meeting. This meeting is our best and perhaps only hope to develop a mutually beneficial business relationship with this new customer. The outcome is not certain; we just need to be certain we do our absolute best.

The Meeting Arrives

You're on the doorstep. Your planning was thorough and you are prepared. The majority of preparation that will determine the success (or lack thereof) of this meeting is done before you will ever see the customer. The meeting is simply the final step in a long process. But if you have prepared deliberately, accurately, and thoroughly, you should be more than ready to execute your plan.

Volumes of published research are available on how to effectively speak, listen, stand, sit, position yourself, look, and interact. After learning and applying the communication models employed by five different biopharma organizations, working with and learning directly from eight different managers and directors, and training hundreds of representatives, I am fairly well-versed in communication strategy. So let's review some high-priority considerations for a mutually beneficial meeting.

Greet your customer professionally with a handshake commensurate to that of your customer. I once shook the hand of a customer with an uncharacteristically feeble grip. Initially I thought this was just her preference, perhaps indicating reticence to meet with me? Several days later, after a mutually productive initial meeting, she emailed me with a question and alluded to a medical condition that caused her to have significant weakness in her hands. Two lessons learned: judging a person by her handshake probably isn't helpful, and adapting your handshake to his or hers is wise for many reasons, not the least of which may be reducing the risk of harming the customer.

Introduce your customer to any colleague you bring with you. If there is a colleague working with you the day of your meeting, perhaps you might also include him and his value to the customer in your planning for that meeting. What value can he or she provide to you and your customer during the meeting? This added human resource can be quite valuable; apply it effectively.

Speak to your customer. Look at his or her eyes during your conversation. Be conscious of where you're looking at any given moment. Everything you do—including where you look—is, ideally, intentional and purposeful (and likely noticed by your customer).

Lead the meeting; after all, you asked for it. Begin with a review of the agenda, incorporating any known customer PINs. Ensure you also inquire as to any additional questions or interests your customer may have at the beginning and throughout the meeting.

Be cognizant of time and use it wisely. If you're uncertain how much time your customer has available, ask him and adhere to the constraint. Be efficient, personable, and thorough while respecting the priorities, interests, and needs of your customer. He may find significant interest in a subject or resource you present, so much so that he prefers to continue your meeting past the initially planned conclusion. If you see your customer has interest in a topic not on your agenda, you may say, "Let's review the steps of that procedure," or "Would you like an overview of the warnings and adverse events?" If the customer appears interested and time is limited, I would probably start with the former and go ahead and present, versus asking permission to do so.

Listen. During my very first training class back in August, 2000, I completed a self-evaluation after my formal assessment. For me, the most important question asked on the form was this: "Did you listen at least 51% of the time?" The short answer? Not even close.

When customers demonstrated more patience with us, thanks in part to our samples, lunches, golf outings, sporting events, copious speaking opportunities, or other incentives, they perhaps tolerated us speaking more than we listened. Today, if you're not listening at least 51% of the time, you're quite possibly engaged in your last meeting with this customer. Stephen Covey said it best, "Seek first to understand, then to be understood."[1]

Take notes. Let's generalize a bit and put interactions with customers into one of two categories: meetings or the notorious "standup." For those not familiar with prototypical pharmaceutical rep communication with HCPs, a "standup" is characterized by a brief greeting, perhaps a question to the HCP with a brief answer, a signature for samples left with the office, and courteous departing salutations. The entire encounter often concludes within 60 seconds.

For substantive meetings, have your agenda written or typed on your computer or tablet. As you progress through the meeting, respect the fact most people will not remember every high-priority detail communicated during this time. We also must respect the value of information our customer is providing. How do we do this? Document information you want to remember. Jot down key points of interest or items requiring further action or inquiry. As much as we all want or intend to remember everything, we probably won't. Take notes.

Conclude the meeting with a summary of action items for you and your customer. Ask any clarifying questions necessary and respectfully and personably close the meeting.

Consider your time to be just as valuable as that of your customers. Thanking your customer for her time implies several of your opinions (most of them negative) regarding your perceived worth or value to your customer. These include: the time you spent together was perhaps not as valuable as time she would have spent otherwise; she is donating time to you; your time is less valuable than hers.

This statement appears to decrease your credibility and perceived value. If you provide genuine value, you received no such gift of time from your customer. You provided her with resources, ideas, and training so she might be more effective in her work. May I suggest you provided each other mutually beneficial value as a result of your meeting? If you genuinely feel the time she "gave" you was worthy of your thanks, you may want to ask yourself, *Did I provide genuine value my customer can apply to help her achieve her desired outcomes? Or was that a one-sided meeting benefitting only me?!*

Follow through on your commitments. Not long ago I received a noteworthy email from a senior clinical leader employed by a large federal health system. We met eight months prior at his request. Our meeting focused on his priorities and how I could help him achieve his objectives. Upon concluding this meeting, we each knew what the other would do. I completed my action items, one of which was sending a follow up email outlining our next steps. Two weeks passed. He didn't reply. I sent another email briefly restating next steps and inquiring as to his status regarding his action items. Three more weeks passed. No reply.

I sent three more messages over the ensuing months with no reply. I eventually spoke with his nurse who informed me of myriad changes since our last meeting. After we spoke, I suspect she perhaps talked with the physician about our conversation. Shortly thereafter (approximately eight months after our initial meeting), he sent a very kind and apologetic email indicating appreciation. For what? My professional persistence. He specifically asked me to do this work for him when we met—so I did, even when he appeared disinterested. For me to become frustrated or be insulted by his non-responsiveness would have been counterproductive. Be *professionally persistent.*

Learn to Ask Great Questions

We said hello, shook hands, sat down, and engaged in brief weekend-reviewing conversation. Then she looked up, right into my eyes, and said, "So, what do you want out of this, Scott? What are your intentions?" No, this wasn't a bad start to a first date. These were the questions posed to me and my representative by a hospitalist (physician) customer I'll call Ingrid, in a health system in California.

Having worked with Ingrid several years earlier, I had a fair understanding of what she valued. However, we hadn't spoken for several years and were just now reconnecting, so my representative and I had much to learn about her current priorities, interests, and needs—and what she perceived as *genuine value.*

Her questions were assertive and forthright and I utterly respected her candor. An honest customer with a purpose is something to value highly in this profession. And she wanted to know our motives.

As a district manager leading 12 representatives responsible for promoting a product in hospitals within large health systems, one of my perhaps obvious motives was growing appropriate business. She wanted to hear me say it. And, more importantly, she wanted to hear how my representative and I were going to do it; how we were going to grow business by working with her and her colleagues and at the same time help her get what *she* wanted. Bottom line: she wanted to know how we were going to provide her genuine value.

Ingrid had some of the most desirable traits I could hope for in a customer: she was willing to work with manufacturer's representatives who provided her genuine value and she knew how to do just that.

Fictitious sports marketing agent Jerry McGuire, played by Tom Cruise in the like-named movie, said it best: "Help me help you." Jerry was working hard to get his client to apply the advice he was imparting as this would serve the client's (very pronounced) personal interests. Jerry could provide value to his client but knew, unless his client responded to him, those resources would go unapplied.[2]

Jerry's frustrations echo the frustrations of many biopharma vendors today. We often have resources of substantial value but, due to customer reticence to communicate their real priorities, interests, and/or needs (or communicate at all), those resources often remain unapplied. **Asking effective questions after earning some trust and demonstrating potential value can be the catalyst to your customers ultimately helping themselves with your resources, thus leading to better outcomes for all involved.**

The Power of the Question

As we've already established, health care providers and their leaders, with whom vendors want to communicate, are less interested than ever in speaking with us. The reality is, though, if we ask effective questions, customers will tell us their priorities, their interests, and even their needs.

Effective questions are usually open questions. A closed question typically begins with words such as *Is, Are, Do, Will.* They lead to brief "yes" or "no "answers. Open questions, on the other hand, typically begin with words such as *What, Why*, and *How*. They can elicit answers that provide far greater information. Commit those three words to memory: *what, why, how*. Starting a question with one of those words can make your customers think. The results of their thought processes can be insightful and provide information you can then correlate with your resources.

Did you feel that? By getting your customer to think, you just crossed over from irrelevant to relevant and potentially value-adding. You are now on track to be a resource to your customer, and it all started with a simple question.

"That's it? All I have to do is ask Dr. Misty some questions, she'll tell me what's important to her, and then I can align my resources with her interests and provide value! Hurray!" If only it were that simple.

One company I know of advocated its representatives learn their customers' goals. "Learn their goals, and then you can sell to those goals." They also advocated reps learn this by asking, "What are your goals?"

Sit back for a second and ask yourself that question. What are *your* goals? Take a minute and think about some of your goals.

What went through your head for the last 60 seconds? For me, it was mostly more questions. *Goals for what? Personal goals? Professional goals? Short-term or long-term? Career goals or around a certain project/responsibility? Why am I asking myself this?*

When I coached one of my teams to ask this question, we frequently met the same types of responses: "What kind of goals? I don't have any specific goals. What do you mean? I have all sorts of goals."

Even though this question may seem direct, it and similar questions have two limitations. First, the question is too broad; it needs to be more narrow in scope to uncover information that will assist you. Second, the timing of the question can limit its effectiveness. Even a more refined question will only generate information if your customer has a certain degree of trust in you. Ask this type of open question prematurely and you're likely to receive only shallow or limited answers.

So the **first step in asking open questions is to earn some degree of trust** from your customer. The **second step is crafting a question** focused on specific information that, if received, will help you help your customer get what she wants.

Formulating Questions

Your reading thus far includes the topic of PINs so perhaps I should explain them in more detail here. A helpful tactic I employed over the years to make my questions more concise and focused is to think in terms of customer **priorities, interests, and needs** (PINs). To unpack this idea, let's start at the back of this list, with the needs.

Needs. The need is your customer's "oxygen"; it's the have-to-have. They have to be at the meeting called by their department chair at 2:00 pm. They have to finish the research paper they're writing as the final draft is due in 10 days. They have to reduce their prescribing of branded medications to less than ten percent, as their colleagues have already done (if they don't comply, it may be noted in their annual performance review).

Customer needs may include meeting revenue forecasts, achieving improved outcomes, improving CG-CAHPS™ or H-CAHPS™ scores, conducting safe operations, making payroll, or increasing shareholder value. Help a customer meet a need and you are unquestionably providing genuine value.

Interests. When customers' needs are, or will be, met, they can move on to their interests. An "interest" is defined as a quality that attracts your attention and makes you want to learn more about something or to be involved in something.[3] This term is particularly relevant, given our ever-increasing need not only to demonstrate the value of our products, but also to promote them by effectively weaving them into the fabric of our customer's regular work. Biopharma manufacturers must respond to their customers' interests to be relevant. Without relevance, we are simply a nuisance. And many manufacturers simply have too much to offer the health care consumer for them to be relegated to irrelevance.

At this point, a critical step opens. Which of your customer's interests and needs can you assist in meeting? You cannot help your customer write a research paper, nor can you ensure she is at her meeting on time. You may, however, have the means to provide resources and assistance in discharge counseling of any patients who have been treated with your therapy or device. This may promote better patient outcomes.

If a clinic manager wants to decrease cancelled appointments, you may be able to help with this if reasons for cancellation are determined. Some patients will cancel appointments if they feel the copay, coinsurance, or deductible makes the out-of-pocket cost intolerably high. Patient savings programs can significantly reduce patients' costs, increasing the likelihood they will continue therapy and possibly result in fewer cancellations. Your opportunity is how to integrate the savings program into the treatment process—a beautiful opportunity for a savvy biopharma representative to provide genuine value based on a customer's interest.

Priorities. Once you determine a customer's interest or need, you can assess its priority to your customer. This will, in turn, help you adjust your work accordingly. For example, understanding the priorities of a health system will help you make decisions about how and when to work with customers, and particularly leaders, in that system.

An academic health system I work with is currently poised to significantly expand one of its clinics. I had an opportunity to support two of the leaders in this clinic by connecting them to world-renowned experts in another academic health system across the country. Yet my customers faced a constraint. The end of their fiscal year was quickly approaching and, after that date, there would be no travel budget. One of the leaders was also going on vacation. This left me with a two-day window of opportunity to make everything come together.

I quickly changed my work priorities to accommodate my customers' priorities. The result: with some help, I managed to get it scheduled. They completed the very informative trip before the fiscal year end. They gathered myriad valuable information applicable to them, their patients and staff, and, consequently, the health system.

Adapting and prioritizing based on your customer's micro and macro priorities is a skill set worthy of greater analysis and study as it's absolutely essential to a representative's success.

To provide genuine value, you must align your product not just with your customers' priorities and interests, but ideally with their most fundamental needs. The question then is how to get HCPs and their leaders to share their PINs with you.

The Value of an Open Question

When you seek to understand the PINs of your customers, you'll be well-served to ask specific, open questions. Here are some examples of effective open questions:

- *To an orthopedic surgeon:* "What one or two metrics are most of interest to you regarding your hip replacements?"
- *To a clinic or health services manager:* "What are your top two business priorities for 2017?"

- *To a headache specialist:* "What are the top two outcomes you want to achieve when treating patients with chronic migraine headaches?"
- *To a pharmacoeconomist:* "What two outcomes associated with MS treatment vs. cost of that treatment are you assessing most intricately now and why those particular outcomes?"

Note the specificity in these questions. Ask a general question and you're likely to get a general answer. Then you have to ask another question. Ask a more specific question and you can expect a more specific answer. This is where knowing your customer's work environment, background, or any additional relevant information (fellowship training or other specific interests) may assist you in formulating relevant questions.

Specific, insightful questions can also eliminate a need for more questions. No customer wants to be interviewed, least of all because of poor representative preparation or questioning technique. Specific questions that, when answered, can help you quickly align your resources to client priorities make effective use of your time with your client, something he or she will genuinely appreciate.

How do you assemble these questions? Know all you can about your customer:

- Understand your customer's business environment.
- Think from your customer's perspective. Is she in a senior leadership position or a new fellow? Is he a five-year veteran in clinical care or a 35-year veteran focused on research? Is she self-employed or employed by a large national health system?
- Determine the "health" and situation of his or her employer. Is it growing? Contracting? About to acquire another group? About to be purchased by another system? Hiring? Layoffs

imminent? Every one of these has occurred in my area of responsibility in just the last 18 months.

- Read the website of the customer's employer, particularly the "About" section. Learn when the system was "born," by whom, and what are its core values, current projects, initiatives, or priorities.
- Perform a search of the customer's employer and see what articles emerge in local, regional, or national publications.
- Talk to your friends, neighbors, and local family members to gain insight into your accounts. Be respectful of corporate compliance and confidentiality requirements as well as ethical business practices, as these requirements are frequently policy for biopharma manufacturers as well as our customers.
- Understand the macro-level business drivers of your customers: the Affordable Care Act (ACA), Veterans Affairs policies, changes to your product tiering or formulary status by health plans, etc.
- Understand the general expectations of your customer's role [e.g., chief of group, department chair, dean, staff physician, locum tenens (temporary) physicians, resident, fellow, nurse, physician assistant, advanced registered nurse practitioner, national expert, international expert, etc.]
- Know how others in the clinic or hospital speak of the customer with whom you're planning to talk. Is the person driven? Focused? Nonchalant? Skeptical? Enthusiastic? Apathetic? Upwardly-mobile?

Knowing some background information on your customer is step one in assembling questions. Step two is being very clear about what you want to know. Only then can you ask the question with the potential to produce the information you require.

Suppose you are getting ready to meet with a client and read in her group practice newsletter her clinic has a top priority this year of improving the cardiovascular outcomes in patients with Type 2 diabetes. Your therapy happens to be particularly relevant to these patients and you have some resources to assist her patients, her, and her clinic in a variety of ways.

Your question may start like this, "I understand cardiovascular outcomes of your patients with Type 2 diabetes are a particular priority for the clinic this year." Then you would follow up with a question that addressed a need, interest, or priority:

- *Need Question*: "What two or three priorities do you need to address this year to achieve the outcomes you want related to this metric?"
- *Interest Question:* "What are your particular interests around this outcome measure?"
- *Priorities Question:* "What actions can you take that you see as most relevant in the near term to affect these outcomes?"

Learn in advance what you can about your customer. Then be clear about what you want to know. Finally, formulate a specific, succinct question. Attend to these steps in detail and you're likely to generate two outcomes: 1) improved credibility, since effective questioning requires knowledge and preparation, and, 2) a useful understanding of your customer's PINs such that you may now align your resources to help her achieve her desired outcomes.

Keep the Customer Engaged

When your questions are smartly refined and you know what you want to ask, remember that you're not conducting an interview—relentless questioning is one-sided and selfish. Your work is about helping your customer achieve his or her objectives as well as your own. It's not just about you achieving your objectives. As you create an effective conversation, keep these points in mind:

- Silence and stow your mobile phone. At that moment, nothing is more important than the person in front of you.
- Listen to your customer. Think about her responses from her point of view.
- Focus only on the person sitting in front of you. If your mind wanders, breathe, and bring your thoughts gently back to the conversation.
- Adapt your style to your customer. If she speaks faster than you, you might pick up your pace somewhat; if the customer is more quiet and reserved than you, you may consider communicating more quietly.

Learning the priorities, interests, and needs of your customers happens when you pay attention to the bigger picture when talking with them. One element of this bigger picture is nonverbal communication. Based on thousands of conversations with customers, the following are my guidelines regarding nonverbal communication.

If your customer appears disinterested, she probably is. Looking away, looking at a cell phone, staring out a window, or slouching in a chair can all indicate disinterest. Perhaps a simple, astute question from you is all that's needed to get her re-engaged. Maybe you need to add inflection to your speech. Whatever you do, a change is probably needed.

If a customer is overtly disinterested (e.g., writing in a chart or initiating conversation with someone else), you need to change your approach immediately. You may need to retreat and regroup. Quickly attempt to re-engage the customer or ask to reschedule the meeting. It's important to remember that your time is valuable, too, so don't permit yourself to be marginalized by a customer in this way and not take control of the situation. If you don't assert some control, your relevance may take a big step backwards in the customer's eyes. Be clear and be candid. And, most importantly, be relevant. Here's a sample approach: "Doc, it appears we might benefit from rescheduling this meeting; how about tomorrow or Wednesday during the lunch hour?"

What you want and need are customers actively engaged, participating in the conversation, looking at you, asking insightful questions, and taking notes. Always a helpful technique: self-assess after your conversations to evaluate your effectiveness and identify one adjustment you could make to increase your effectiveness in future meetings.

Open Your Eyes and Tell Me What You See

Understanding the PINs of your customers comes from looking at the whole picture. Even when you prepared your questions, you may need to change on the fly based on what you see in front of you when you actually get to the meeting.

Look at your customer's surroundings to garner some insights that are readily available. In 2001, a physician in private practice told his receptionist to invite me back to his office. I complied to find quite a relaxed environment. He offered me a seat and then a cigar, followed by an offer to spark it up. I declined but he heaved away on his havana. His office was less than tidy. Moments before, from the freezer in his hallway, he had removed some salmon he caught over the weekend (he gave it to a patient). A (quite necessary) shirt button was noticeably absent. He swore often and had little interest in discussing anything at all pertaining to my products, resources, or even the relevant disease states.

Then there was a specialist in my area whose immaculate desk had only a writing pad, a very expensive pen, and a computer monitor. On the credenza, beautifully framed medical training and certification documents flanked a picture of his wife and two children. I suspected I might benefit from approaching him differently than the fisherman-doctor-fashionista.

Some customers, like the cigar-puffing, disinterested, overly jovial fellow, desire copious informal chit-chat prior to any business discussion (which in his case was ultimately limited anyway as he unfortunately demonstrated little interest in optimizing his work). Others, like the highly-organized, detail-oriented, and academically inclined specialist, prefer clear, direct, and succinct communication.

Look at what people choose to wear or drive. Are they wearing an expensive or frugal watch? Do you have any information on what she drives? A Tesla or a 2002 Honda Accord? Some of these elements may communicate your customers' interests or priorities. At a minimum, they may provide you an interesting topic of conversation outside of business. Not every customer, nor do I, wants to talk all business all the time.

Look at how the office is appointed. Are there ornate furnishings or decorations? Or could the furniture stand to be replaced 10 years ago? What level of professionalism and customer service do the staff offer—a model office or one in need of serious training? Is the doctor always running late or regularly right on schedule? All of these elements can communicate attributes of your customer that may help you discern his or her priorities, interests, and needs.

Throughout this process, a word of caution for you: don't assume too much when taking in all this information. (Have you, or someone you know, ever regrettably asked a perhaps slightly overweight woman when she is due?) Information you derive in this way constitutes only data points that may help assemble a more accurate picture of customer's PINs. There is no substitute for face-to-face discussion to determine accurate information.

One final point: if you don't know their interests and they won't respond to your communication attempts, start "casting lines into the water." Many of my successful attempts at communicating with customers who did not know me at all were the result of this work.

I'd mention a training course we're offering, a patient cost-savings program perhaps of interest, training models I have, instruction I can provide, instruction national experts can provide, or simply a clinical update on a recent indication and/or safety information revisions. You need to put something out there that might interest your customer.

Even then, so many customers are so skeptical of our intentions that you might never get a reply. Apply the suggestions in this chapter and this book and you will definitely improve your chances at success.

A multi-modal approach including detailed research, effective planning, astute questions, and assessment of non-verbals and the physical environment all contribute to your ability to discern customer priorities, interests, and needs. Perception, inquiry, and analysis will provide the savvy biopharma vendor many data points that ultimately coalesce into understanding what tangible work you can do and/or resources you can provide to consequently bring value to your customer. These will make you not just relevant but *genuinely valuable*—the key to developing your business.

10
Be the Representative Who Stands Out

*True generosity lies in striving so that these hands—
whether of individuals or entire people— need be extended
less and less in supplication, so that more and more they
become human hands which work and, working,
transform the world.*
—Paulo Freire

Early in my field management days, I witnessed some "best practices" that built unparalleled value and success for one of my reps who differentiated himself from his peers in consistently positive and noteworthy ways. One of Andy's many skills was his attention to detail, notably during his post-call (meeting) documenting. After a meeting, adamant and deliberate about this next step, he would sit in a quiet place free from distraction and document all he hadn't already noted during the meeting. He would also note or confirm any actions he was to take post-meeting and when he would act. This process aided his effectiveness in numerous ways.

Andy worked in Portland, Oregon, a notoriously anti-biopharma, anti-representative, limited-access MSA. He was the first in my district to achieve a major business milestone—a large hospital using our primary product and device throughout all relevant departments. A project like this took many months as the stakeholders were varied and numerous. I recall working with Andy when he was several months into the initiative and progress was stalling.

Andy took to his notes—pages and pages of notes—in his smartphone. Several pages into these notes, he found some text outlining a contact he hadn't followed up with. He contacted this customer again and earned a productive meeting with her, catalyzing additional steps that eventually led to substantial progress. Had he not been so deliberate with his note-taking, achieving his ultimate objective might have been less than plausible.

Similarly well-served by Andy's attention to detail were the written business updates he sent me monthly—consistently the most detailed, robust, and clear updates any team member supplied me. Each of his accounts was dissected in relevant detail. The status of each key area of his business was regularly updated.

His attention to detail was also evident in his work when I was with him. Most members of my team knew their accounts in similar detail, but Andy put his in writing. Therefore, he had a reference library that held the details he may have otherwise forgotten. These details proved consistently beneficial to Andy in more ways than I can cite here.

To this point, you've read much around planning meetings but little on strategic business planning or the all-important *business updates* our leaders often require. These updates are the documented work, results, and account-status updates we produce according to the business plan we developed for a particular customer, account, or territory.

It's difficult to overstate the value of this document to a representative and the first-line manager/director. This value comes in many forms, including business development, accountability, aligning resources to customer's PINs, and building definite connections with customers. All of these can significantly improve our communication effectiveness and corresponding value delivery.

This is why one of your best practices in this business will be your consistent attention to your written business updates (BU). Being accountable to provide your leaders regular (monthly is often sufficient) written business updates keeps us focused, thinking, planning, executing, accountable, and deliberate in the process of serving our employers and our customers.

A robust BU can take two to three hours to update well and three to four hours to update quite thoroughly with refined detail and plausible, aligned action items. Understand, this is time very well-spent. I learned that rushing through a BU can serve to limit future potential business development. Attend to it regularly and refer back to it often and you may find your business develops just a bit faster like Andy's did.

Be the One Representative They Want to Meet

Based on the conversations my colleagues and I have with our customers, it's a minute number of representatives with which HCPs and their leaders meet in a given week, month, or even year. In fact, over the last year when I asked several customers, "How many representatives do you meet with in a given month?" all the replies I received were similar. Here are a few:

> "Aside from the occasional DME rep, no one except you."
>
> "It's been about three years since I met with a rep."
>
> (pointing at me) "About one."
>
> "You mean in a year? One. You."
>
> "I haven't seen a rep since I finished my fellowship three years ago."
>
> (laughing) "I haven't met with a rep in 10 years."

I provide you those comments at the risk of sounding boastful when my intention is quite the opposite. Applying my skill set for a customer-focused organization is what allows me to connect with these customers and ultimately help them. I worked with five different biopharma companies and only twice enjoyed a company culture and products that enabled me and my colleagues to be sufficiently effective and productive. And, in speaking with friends and former colleagues scattered throughout dozens of companies nationwide, these two conditions don't appear to be prevalent in biopharma. But they do exist.

I also expect, as more doors close to vendor reps across the US, many more organizations will be forced to acknowledge what some already know: we have to increase the *genuine value* (as defined by our customers) that our representatives provide those they serve. And that value is most often optimally communicated and demonstrated during in-person meetings.* Otherwise, it will be only a short time before the doors are completely closed.

If you connected with a customer and are in process of providing him value, well done! You distinguished yourself from the masses. You made a wise choice to join your organization and represent the products and services you're responsible for. You found a company culture genuinely *connected* to the priorities, interests, and needs of your customers.

As a result, the doctor will see you now because she is deriving specific and genuine resources of value to her, her employer, and/or her patients.

The Road Often Travelled

My father gave me a copy of M. Scott Peck's well-known work *The Road Less Travelled* when I graduated from college. His timing was right on as I departed the confines of university and ventured out into the world of complete independence. I was on my own and what

* Connection via phone, email, text, etc. are options as well but less effective than in-person meetings.

better fact to know at this point than the first sentence in Peck's book: "Life is difficult."[1] The book highlights the many challenges we as humans may face in our lifetime. It also suggests steps to help us grow as a result of those challenges.

Contrary to the title of Peck's fine work, I hope the path I've laid out in this book will become for biopharma representatives who read it "the road MOST travelled." Hopefully you now have a better understanding of the effective biopharma vendor, the environment we work in, and how we can serve our clients with our products and services such that they achieve the clinical and business outcomes they desire. I also hope you see there are specific steps you can take to be effective in your work today and tomorrow.

The doctor *will* see you now. Understand, if you have a valued product or service, a company culture that supports its field organization effectively, and you have connected with a customer (i.e., you have found a way to align your resources with her priorities, interests, or needs), you are well on your way to sustaining a mutually beneficial clinical and business relationship. You are not one of many but one of a few to distinguish herself as a business leader working for the mutual best interest of her customers and her employer. You respect the quote by George Merck II found at the beginning of Chapter One in this book:

We try never to forget that medicine is for the people.
It is not for profits.
The profits follow, and if we have remembered that,
they never fail to appear.
The better we have remembered it,
the larger they have been.

You relentlessly focus on the patient and how he/she will be best served by your customer with your products and resources.

You know what patients like, want, and need. How do you know this? You are or possibly were a patient at some point yourself. Or you have family members requiring health care services. We are all closely connected to the genuine value HCPs can provide their patients. And now we are uniquely suited to help them provide even greater value to their employers, to our friends, our family members, and all the patients they serve.

In Closing

One of my intentions in writing this book is to help those of us still in this business to restore trustworthiness to our industry in the eyes of our most reticent customers. In past years, we unfortunately decimated our worth in the eyes of many customers, particularly in the late 90s and early 2000s. When the biopharma representative majority are recognized in all MSAs as regularly providing genuine value—and consequently, are recognized as credible, trustworthy, and respected partners to our customers—I will be satisfied that we repaired our reputation. I aspire for this generation of biopharma manufacturers and representatives to be recognized as the one that did more good for our customers and their patients than any predecessor group. It's in our universal best interest as an industry to think and work this way every single day.

I welcome your insights, suggestions, and related topics you feel might be worthy of study. Several references in this book show statistics for the entire US market. I also spoke with dozens of colleagues and referred back to work done with several others from my past. Still, these insights represent just a sample of the population. Ideally, I'd like to receive specific insights spanning several therapeutic areas on every market in the United States. If we are to collectively achieve the vision of restoring our industry's credibility, trustworthiness, and value, we need to share relevant insights with one another as to how best we can achieve this objective.

Tell me about your MSA, your account types, and what you experienced over the years—the helpful, the hindering, and the perplexing. What's changed dramatically in your MSA over the last five, ten, or fifteen years? How are you building mutually beneficial business partnerships today? What is the genuine value you provide your customers? What is your most significant impedance to feeling gratified by the work you perform daily? What do you want most from the work you do every day, year after year? As always, ensure you adhere to your employer's policies relating to confidential information protection.

Finally, our work is not just about dollars. It's about developing business in a healthy and mutually productive way. Most conversations I've had with representatives in the recent past focus on their innate and deep desire to be valued for their positive impact on customer results, outcomes, achievements, etc. We have a deep desire to provide substantive and genuine value that ultimately makes a positive difference for those with whom we work as well as those they may treat. We want more from our work than money, completing four to six meetings per day, or dropping off three boxes of samples.

May we part ways at this point by reading some insight from Josiah Royce, a Harvard philosopher who wrote about what and why we seek more from life than merely being sheltered, clothed, and fed. He wrote of a fundamental human need to serve something greater than ourselves. According to Royce, this is the opposite of individualism, a trait he called "loyalty," which "solves the paradox of our ordinary existence by showing us outside of ourselves the cause which is to be served, and inside of ourselves the will which delights to do this service, and which is not thwarted but enriched and expressed in such service."[2]

We all need to work, and to know our work has impact and serves others in meaningful ways. We want work that makes us part of something greater than ourselves. We want to be *loyal*. By understanding our mistakes and their impact on our customers, by providing relevant and genuine value while representing a company culture truly dedicated to the customers we serve, and by focusing our work on aligning our resources with customer priorities, interests, and needs, we can be the loyal ones. We can be the trusted, respected biopharma vendor representatives our customers truly value—and the one doctors will see, trust and value.

GLOSSARY

A clarifying distinction between the terms "biologic," "biopharmaceutical," and "drug" may be helpful here. You see definitions of these and other relevant terms below. To simplify this nomenclature "stew" and align us on current use of these terms, here is a brief summary: biologics are often complex molecules consisting of one or many proteins; drugs (or chemical substances) usually refer to small-molecule products (chemicals) and are not a biological substance.[1] The term "biopharma" as applied in this book, refers to both biologics and drug manufacturers.

Attending – Clinical faculty are usually staff physicians at a given medical school's affiliated teaching hospitals and clinics. They treat patients, teach future physicians, and in many cases, conduct research. In their hospital roles, these doctors are referred to as attending physicians. They oversee the work of residents and fellows—medical school graduates pursuing advanced education in a medical or surgical specialty. They also instruct medical students on their way to earning M.D. degrees.[2]

Biologic – Any virus, therapeutic serum, toxin, antitoxin, or analogous product applicable to the prevention, treatment or cure of diseases or injuries of man.[3]

Biopharma – the industry researching, developing, manufacturing, and occasionally commercializing both biologics and drugs.

Biopharmaceutical – noun: a pharmaceutical product manufactured by biotechnology methods (involving live organisms; bioprocessing).[4]

Brand – The marketing practice of creating a name, symbol, or design that identifies and differentiates a product from other products. An effective brand strategy gives you a major edge in increasingly competitive markets.[5]

CAHPS™ – Consumer Assessment of Healthcare Providers and Systems (CAHPS™) surveys ask consumers and patients to report on and evaluate their experiences with health care. These surveys cover topics that are important to consumers and focus on aspects of quality that consumers are best qualified to assess, such as the communication skills of providers and ease of access to health care services. All CAHPS™ surveys and related guidance documents are free to anyone who wants to use these surveys to assess patients' experiences with care. Users of CAHPS™ survey results include patients and consumers, health care providers' quality monitors and regulators, health plans, community collaboratives, and public and private purchasers of health care. These individuals and organizations use the survey results to evaluate and compare health care providers and to improve the quality of health care services. Surveys are available from the Agency for Healthcare Research and Quality (AHRQ), a federal agency within the US Dept. of Health and Human Services:

American Indian
Clinician & Group (CG-CAHPS™)
Dental Plan
Experience of Care and Health Outcomes (ECHO)
Health Plan
Home Health Care
Hospice
Hospital (Adult Hospital Survey and Child Hospital Survey)
In-Center Hemodialysis Survey
Nursing Home
Outpatient and Ambulatory Surgery[6]

Center for Medicare and Medicaid Services (CMS) – a federal agency within the United States Department of Health and Human Services (HHS). This agency runs the Medicare, Medicaid, and Children's Health Insurance Programs (CHIP), and the federally facilitated Marketplace.[7]

Drug – therapeutic agent; any substance, other than food, used in the prevention, diagnosis, alleviation, treatment, or cure of disease.[8]

Fellow – Physicians who seek more specialized training after their residencies may pursue fellowships. For example, a doctor who intends to specialize in cancer treatment may complete an internal medicine residency followed by an oncology fellowship. Physicians in these programs are referred to as fellows.[9]

Formulary – an official list of drugs approved for prescription or administration to patients of a hospital or health maintenance organization (HMO) or to beneficiaries of a health insurance program, or to residents of Canadian provinces that use such an instrument.[10]

Health Care Provider (HCP) – any individual, institution, or agency that provides health services to health care consumers.[11] (In this book I most frequently employ this term referring to an individual person providing health care.)

Health Maintenance Organization (HMO) – "pre-paid" or "capitated" insurance plans in which individuals or their employers pay a fixed monthly fee for services instead of a separate charge for each visit or service. The monthly fees remain the same, regardless of types or levels of services provided. Services are provided by physicians who are employed by or under contract with the HMO. HMOs vary in design. Depending on the type of the HMO, services may be provided in a central facility or in a physician's own office.[12]

Integrated Delivery Network (IDN) – also known as an Integrated Delivery System, a formal system of providers and sites of care that provides both health care services and a health insurance plan to patients in a particular geographic area.[13]

Intern – the first year of postgraduate medical education is sometimes called an internship, although this term is no longer used as widely as in the past. An intern (not to be confused with internist, the term for a physician who practices internal medicine) or a first-year resident is a recent medical school graduate who is just starting specialty training.[14]

Medical Student – In general, the medical school curriculum in the first two years stresses both factual knowledge and key skills such as critical thinking, establishing rapport with patients and colleagues, and conducting medical histories and physical examinations. In the final two years of medical school, students rotate through clerkships in both primary care and specialty medicine, applying what they have learned in the classroom to supervised experiences with real patients. During their education, students must take the United States Medical Licensing Examination (USMLE), a three-step test all potential physicians must pass in order to practice medicine in the United States and Canada. The first step—which covers basic medical principles—comes near the end of the second year of medical school, followed by the next step—on clinical diagnosis and disease development—in the fourth year. A final step on clinical management is usually taken during the first or second year of residency.[15]

Metropolitan Statistical Area (MSA) – Metropolitan Statistical Areas have at least one urbanized area of 50,000 or more population, plus adjacent territory that has a high degree of social and economic integration with the core as measured by commuting ties.

Micropolitan Statistical Areas–a new set of statistical areas–have at least one urban cluster of at least 10,000 but less than 50,000 population, plus adjacent territory that has a high degree of social and economic integration with the core as measured by commuting ties. Metropolitan and Micropolitan Statistical Areas are defined in terms of whole counties (or equivalent entities).[16] In this book, MSA refers to Metropolitan Statistical Areas.

Patient Protection and Affordable Care Act (PPACA) – the first part of the comprehensive health care reform law enacted on March 23, 2010. The law was amended by the Health Care and Education Reconciliation Act on March 30, 2010. The name "Affordable Care Act" is usually used to refer to the final, amended version of the law. (It's sometimes known as "PPACA," "ACA," or "Obamacare.") The law provides numerous rights and protections that make health coverage more fair and easy to understand, along with subsidies (through "premium tax credits" and "cost-sharing reductions"). The law also expands the Medicaid program to cover more people with low incomes.[17]

Pharmaceutical – a medicinal drug, or relating to or engaged in pharmacy or the manufacture and sale of pharmaceuticals. A pharmaceutical product is generally one that is made up using available chemical compounds.[18]

Preferred Provider Organization (PPO) – a managed care organization of health providers who contract with an insurer or third-party administrator (TPA) to provide health insurance coverage to policy holders represented by the insurer or TPA. Policy holders receive substantial discounts from health care providers who are partnered with the PPO. If policy holders use a physician outside the PPO plan, they typically pay more for the medical care.[19]

Resident – a physician who graduated medical school and has moved on to specialized training in a residency, usually at a hospital. Residency programs vary in length depending on the specialty, but generally last three to five years for initial board certification. Subspecialty training may extend the period to as long as 11 years following the award of the M.D. degree.[20]

ENDNOTES

Preface

1. Wazana, Ashley. "Physicians and the Pharmaceutical Industry: Is a Gift Ever Just a Gift?" *JAMA* 283, no. 3 (January 19, 2000): 373–80.
2. Lexchin, Joel. "Interactions between Physicians and the Pharmaceutical Industry: What Does the Literature Say?" *CMAJ: Canadian Medical Association Journal* 149, no. 10 (November 15, 1993): 1401–7.
3. May, C. D. "Selling Drugs By 'Educating' Physicians." *Journal of Medical Education*. January, 1961.
4. "Pharmaceutical Sales Ban." *The Everett Clinic*. 2016. http://www.everettclinic.com/drugreps. Accessed August 27, 2016.
5. Khedkar, Pratap and Sturgis, Malcom. "AccessMonitor™ 2015 Executive Summary." *ZS Associates*. http://www.zs.com/publications/articles/accessmonitor-2015-executive-summary.aspx. Accessed August 27, 2016.
6. "Savvy." *Dictionary.com,* http://www.dictionary.com/browse/savvy?s=t. Accessed August 27, 2016.
7. Roosevelt, Theodore. *"Citizenship In A Republic."* Speech given by Roosevelt at the University of Paris; Paris, France, April 23, 1910.

Introduction

1. Simon, Paul. *The Sound of Silence*. New York City: Columbia Studios. October, 1964.
2. Sorkin, Aaron. *The American President*. Directed by Reiner, Rob. Produced by Castle Rock Entertainment. Distributed in the USA by Columbia Pictures, 1995.
3. Tirrell, Meg. "Express Scripts, Imprimis to Offer $1 Daraprim Alternative." *CNBC*. December 1, 2015. http://www.cnbc.

com/2015/11/30/express-scripts-imprimis-to-offer-daraprim-alternative.html.

4. "Daraprim Price Jump Raises Concerns among ID Groups, Providers." *Healio Infectious Disease News*. September 17, 2015. http://www.healio.com/infectious-disease/hiv-aids/news/online/%7B745d9cc5-df37-4139-b1ac-6dde7b8ae463%7D/daraprim-price-jump-raises-concerns-among-id-groups-providers.
5. Stone, Kathlyn. "Was Turing Pharmaceuticals' 5000% Price Increase a Tipping Point?" *Health News Review*. October 8, 2015. http://www.healthnewsreview.org/2015/10/was-turing-pharmaceuticals-outrageous-price-increase-a-tipping-point/.
6. Johnson, Carolyn. "Doctors, Hospitals Condemn out-of-Control Drug Prices as Senate Investigation Begins." *Washington Post*. https://www.washingtonpost.com/news/wonk/wp/2015/12/09/doctors-hospitals-condemn-out-of-control-drug-prices-as-senate-investigation-begins/. Accessed August 27, 2016.
7. Pollack, Andrew. "Senators Condemn Big Price Increases for Drugs." *The New York Times*. December 9, 2015. https://www.nytimes.com/2015/12/10/business/senators-condemn-big-price-increases-for-drugs.html.
8. Loftus, Peter. "Drugmakers Raise Prices Despite Criticisms." *Wall Street Journal*. January 10, 2016. https://www.wsj.com/articles/drugmakers-raise-prices-despite-criticisms-1452474210.
9. Ahmedin Jemal, Miller, Kimberly D., and Siegel, Rebecca L. "Cancer Statistics, 2015." *CA: A Cancer Journal for Clinicians* 65, no. 1. February 2015, 5–29.
10. "Ledipasvir-Sofosbuvir (Harvoni) – Treatment." *Hepatitis C Online*. http://www.hepatitisc.uw.edu/page/treatment/drugs/ledipasvir-sofosbuvir. Accessed August 27, 2016.

11. Loftus, Peter. “Gilead Knew Hepatitis Drug Price Was High, Senate Says.” *Wall Street Journal*. December 1, 2015, sec. Business. http://www.wsj.com/articles/gilead-knew-hepatitis-drug-price-was-high-senate-says-1449004771.
12. ProPublica. “New Hepatitis C Drugs Are Costing Medicare Billions.” *Washington Post*. https://www.washingtonpost.com/national/health-science/medicare-spent-45-billion-on-new-hepatitis-c-drugs-last-year-data-shows/2015/03/29/66952dde-d32a-11e4-a62f-ee745911a4ff_story.html. Accessed August 27, 2016.
13. “Health Expenditures.” Centers for Disease Control and Prevention. http://www.cdc.gov/nchs/fastats/health-expenditures.html. Accessed August 27, 2016.
14. *Steve Jobs: The Movie*. DVD. Directed by Danny Boyle. Los Angeles: Legendary Pictures, 2015.

Chapter One

1. Merck George. “Medicine Is for the Patient, Not for the Profits.” Medical College of Virginia at Richmond. December 1, 1950. https://www.merck.com/about/our-people/gw-merck-doc.pdf.
2. AccessMonitor™ 2015 Executive Summary.” ZS Associates. http://www.zsassociates.com/publications/articles/accessmonitor-2015-executive-summary.aspx. Accessed August 27, 2016.
3. “AccessMonitor™ 2015 Executive Summary.” *ZS Associates*. http://www.zsassociates.com/publications/articles/accessmonitor-2015-executive-summary.aspx. Accessed August 27, 2016.
4. “AccessMonitor™ 2014 Executive Summary.” *ZS Associates*. Accessed August 27, 2016. http://www.zsassociates.com/publications/articles/accessmonitor-2014-executive-summary.aspx.

5. Szabo, Liz. "Health Systems Cutting Costs by Closing Door on Drug Reps." *USA Today*. August 25, 2004. http://usatoday30.usatoday.com/educate/college/healthscience/articles/20040829.htm.
6. Wilhelm, Karen. "Hospital Gets Vendor Visits under Control." *Lean Reflections*. August 12, 2009. http://www.leanreflect.com/2009/08/hospital-gets-vendor-visits-under.html.
7. Carroll, Sarah. "Best Practices to Eliminate or Reduce Conflicts of Interest at Academic Medical Centers." *The PEW Charitable Trust*. March 4, 2014. http://www.pewtrusts.org/en/multimedia/data-visualizations/2014/best-practices-to-eliminate-or-reduce-conflicts-of-interest-at-academic-medical-centers.

Chapter Two

1. Frost, Robert. "Mending Wall." n.d.
2. Martinez, Barbara, and Mathews, Anna Wilde. "E-Mails Suggest Merck Knew Vioxx's® Dangers at Early Stage." *Wall Street Journal*, sec. News. November 1, 2004. http://www.wsj.com/articles/SB109926864290160719.
3. Schmidt, Michael S. and Thomas, Katie. "Glaxo Agrees to Pay $3 Billion in Fraud Settlement." *The New York Times*. July 2, 2012. http://www.nytimes.com/2012/07/03/business/glaxosmithkline-agrees-to-pay-3-billion-in-fraud-settlement.html.
4. Mintzes, Barbara, et al. "Pharmaceutical Sales Representatives and Patient Safety: A Comparative Prospective Study of Information Quality in Canada, France, and the United States." *Journal of General Internal Medicine* 28, no. 10. October 2013: 1368–75, doi:10.1007/s11606-013-2411-7.

5. “FDA Estimates Vioxx® Caused 27,785 Deaths.” April 11, 2004. https://www.consumeraffairs.com/news04/vioxx_estimates.html.
6. Martinez, Barbara, and Mathews, Anna Wilde. “E-Mails Suggest Merck Knew Vioxx’s® Dangers at Early Stage.” *Wall Street Journal*, sec. News. November 1, 2004. http://www.wsj.com/articles/SB109926864290160719.
7. Martinez, Barbara, and Mathews, Anna Wilde. “E-Mails Suggest Merck Knew Vioxx’s® Dangers at Early Stage.” *Wall Street Journal*, sec. News. November 1, 2004. http://www.wsj.com/articles/SB109926864290160719.
8. Martinez and Mathews. “E-Mails Suggest Merck Knew Vioxx’s® Dangers at Early Stage.”
9. Schmidt and Thomas. “Glaxo Agrees to Pay $3 Billion in Fraud Settlement.”
10. Kessel, Mark. “Restoring the Pharmaceutical Industry’s Reputation.” *Nature Biotechnology* 32, no. 10. October 2014: 983–90, doi:10.1038/nbt.3036.
11. “Credible.” *Merriam Webster Dictionary*. http://www.merriam-webster.com/dictionary/credible. Accessed August 28, 2016.
12. Groeger, Lena. “Big Pharma’s Big Fines.” *Pro Publica*. February 24, 2014. http://projects.propublica.org/graphics/bigpharma.
13. Smith, Aaron. “Pity the Poor Pharmaceutical Sales Rep.” *CNNMoney.com*. April 4, 2007. http://money.cnn.com/2007/04/02/news/companies/drug_rep/?postversion=2007040406.
14. “Managed Care.” *Medicaid*. https://www.medicaid.gov/medicaid-chip-program-information/by-topics/delivery-systems/managed-care/managed-care-site.html. Accessed August 28, 2016.

15. Merritt, Martin. "Free Drug Samples to Patients Come with Restrictions | Physicians Practice." *Physicians Practice.* November 30, 2014. http://www.physicianspractice.com/blog/free-drug-samples-patients-come-restrictions.
16. "Best Practices for Academic Medical Centers." *Columbia University's Center on Medicine as a Profession.* October 10, 2013. http://imapny.org/wp-content/themes/imapny/File%20Library/Best%20Practice%20toolkits/Best-Practices_Samples.pdf.
17. Pinckney, Richard G. et al. "The Effect of Medication Samples on Self-Reported Prescribing Practices: A Statewide, Cross-Sectional Survey." *Journal of General Internal Medicine* 26, no. 1. January 2011: 40–44, doi:10.1007/s11606-010-1483-x.
18. Engel, Mary, and Lin II, Rong-Gong. "Drug Firms' Freebies Banned." *Los Angeles Times.* September 13, 2006. http://articles.latimes.com/2006/sep/13/local/me-docs13.
19. Hensley, Scott and Martinez, Barbara. "To Sell Their Drugs, Companies Increasingly Rely on Doctors." *Wall Street Journal.* July 15, 2005, sec. News. http://www.wsj.com/articles/SB112138815452186385.
20. Ibid.
21. "How Much Is This Going to Cost Me?" *Healthy It.* November 12, 2014. https://www.healthit.gov/providers-professionals/faqs/how-much-going-cost-me.
22. Harris, Gardiner. "Family Physician Can't Give Away Solo Practice." *The New York Times.* April 22, 2011. http://www.nytimes.com/2011/04/23/health/23doctor.html.

Chapter Three

1. Schultz, Howard and Yang, Dori Jones. *Pour Your Heart Into It: How Starbucks Built a Company One Cup at a Time.* New York: Hachette Books, 1999.

2. “Corporate Integrity Agreements,” *Office of Inspector General, U.S. Department of Health and Human Services.* Accessed August 28, 2016. https://oig.hhs.gov/compliance/corporate-integrity-agreements/.
3. Pink, Dan. “The Puzzle of Motivation.” July 24, 2009. http://www.ted.com/talks/dan_pink_on_motivation?language=en.
4. Gladwell, Malcolm. *Outliers: The Story of Success*. New York: Back Bay Books, 2011
5. Rockoff, Jonathan, “As Doctors Lose Clout, Drug Firms Redirect the Sales Call.” *The Wall Street Journal,* September 24, 2014.
6. http://www.fiercebiotech.com/special-report/1-pfizer-top-5-layoffs-of-2007
7. Weintraub, Arlene. “The Doctor Won’t See You Now.” *Bloomberg*. Accessed August 28, 2016. http://www.bloomberg.com/news/articles/2007-02-04/the-doctor-wont-see-you-now.
8. Rockoff, Jonathan, “As Doctors Lose Clout, Drug Firms Redirect the Sales Call.” *The Wall Street Journal,* September 24, 2014
9. Pink. “The Puzzle of Motivation.”

Chapter Four

1. Tzu, Sun. *The Art Of War*. Filiquarian, n.d.
2. “AccessMonitor™ 2014 Executive Summary.”
3. Abelson, Reed, and Creswell, Julie. “New Laws and Rising Costs Create a Surge of Supersizing Hospitals.” *The New York Times*. August 12, 2013. http://www.nytimes.com/2013/08/13/business/bigger-hospitals-may-lead-to-bigger-bills-for-patients.html.
4. Wilde Mathews, Anna. “Health-Care Providers, Insurers Supersize.” *Wall Street Journal*. September 21, 2015, sec. Business. http://www.wsj.com/articles/health-care-providers-insurers-supersize-1442850400.

5. Harris, "Family Physician Can't Give Away Solo Practice."
6. Engelberg, J., "Financial Conflicts of Interest in Medicine," P. 1 and Figure 2, January, 2014.
7. Engelberg, J., "Financial Conflicts of Interest in Medicine," Figure 3, January, 2014
8. Engelberg, J., "Financial Conflicts of Interest in Medicine," Figure 4, January, 2014.

Chapter Seven

1. Powers, Mike et al. "Quarterbacks, Orchestrators, Air Traffic Controllers: The New Activity Plan for Pharma Reps | ZS Associates." http://www.zsassociates.com/publications/whitepapers/the-new-activity-plan-for-pharma-reps.aspx. Accessed August 28, 2016.
2. Ibid.
3. "Succinct." *Merriam Webster Dictionary*. http://www.merriam-webster.com/dictionary/succinct. Accessed August 28, 2016.
4. Carl Elliott, "The Drug Pushers," *The Atlantic,* April 2006, http://www.theatlantic.com/magazine/archive/2006/04/the-drug-pushers/304714/.

Chapter Eight

1. Meilinger, Phillip. "When the Fortress Went Down." *Air Force Magazine*. October 2004. http://www.airforcemag.com/MagazineArchive/pages/2004/october%20 2004/1004fortress.aspx.
2. Gawande, Atul. *The Checklist Manifesto: How to Get Things Right*. New York: Picador, 2011.
3. Enochs, Tim. "One Degree Off Course." *Irrefutable Success*. April 2, 2010. http://www.irrefutablesuccess.com/2010/04/one-degree-off-course/.

4. "Washington State House Final Bill Report - ESHB 2876." House Committee on Health Care & Wellness, n.d. http://lawfilesext.leg.wa.gov/biennium/2009-10/Pdf/Bill%20Reports/House/2876-S.E%20HBR%20FBR%2010.pdf.
5. Covey, Stephen R. *The 7 Habits of Highly Effective People*. New York: Free Press, 1990.

Chapter Nine

1. Ibid.
2. Geoffrey, James. "Train Your Sales Team with Wayne Turmel: How to Ask the Questions That Matter." *Selling Power*. Accessed August 28, 2016. http://www.sellingpower.com/content/article/?a=7043/train-your-sales-team-with-wayne-turmel-how-to-ask-the-questions-that-matter.
3. "Interest." *Merriam Webster Dictionary*. Accessed August 28, 2016. http://www.merriam-webster.com/dictionary/interest.

Chapter Ten

1. Peck, M. Scott. *The Road Less Traveled: A New Psychology of Love, Traditional Values and Spiritual Growth*. New York: Touchstone, 2012.
2. Royce, Josiah. *The Philosophy of Loyalty*. HardPress Publishing, 2013.

Glossary

1. Rader, Ronald A. "What is a Biopharmaceutical?" *BioExecutive International*. March 2005.
2. Association of American Medical Colleges. https://www.aamc.org/download/68806/data/road-doctor.pdf. Accessed November 6, 2016.
3. Rader, Ronald A. What is a Biopharmaceutical? *BioExecutive International*. March 2005.

4. Rader, Ronald A. What is a Biopharmaceutical? *BioExecutive International*. March 2005.
5. https://www.google.com/search?client=safari&rls=en&q=brand+in+marketing+definition&ie=UTF-8&oe=UTF-8, Accessed November 6, 2016.
6. AHRQ site, http://www.ahrq.gov/cahps/about-cahps/index.html. Accessed November 6, 2016.
7. https://www.healthcare.gov/glossary/centers-for-medicare-and-medicaid-services/. Accessed November 6, 2016.
8. Stedman's Online. http://www.stedmansonline.com/content.aspx?id=mlrD1800001694&termtype=t. Accessed November 6, 2016.
9. Association of American Medical Colleges. https://www.aamc.org/download/68806/data/road-doctor.pdf. Accessed November 6, 2016.
10. Stedman's Online,. http://stedmansonline.com/content.aspx?id=mlrF1500004112&termtype=t. Accessed November 6, 2016.
11. Mosby's Medical Dictionary, 8th edition. S.v. "health care provider." http://medical-dictionary.thefreedictionary.com/health+care+provider. Accessed November 6, 2016.
12. https://www.healthinsurance.org/glossary/health-maintenance-organizations-hmos/, accessed 11-6-16.13
13. https://www.google.com/search?client=safari&rls=en&q=integrated+delivery+network+definition&ie=UTF-8&oe=UTF-8. Accessed November 6, 2016.
14. Association of American Medical Colleges. https://www.aamc.org/download/68806/data/road-doctor.pdf. Accessed November 6, 2016.
15. Association of American Medical Colleges. https://www.aamc.org/download/68806/data/road-doctor.pdf. Accessed November 6, 2016.

16. Nussle, Jim. "Update of Statistical Area Definitions and Guidance on Their Uses." Office of Management and Budget. pp. 1–2. Nov 20, 2008.
17. https://www.healthcare.gov/glossary/patient-protection-and-affordable-care-act/. Accessed November 6, 2016.
18. Pharmaceutical Drug Manufacturers web site – accessed 10/17/16, http://www.pharmaceutical-drug-manufacturers.com/pharmaceutical-glossary/glossary-of-terms-p.html.
19. https://www.healthinsurance.org/glossary/preferred-provider-organization-ppo/. Accessed November 6, 2016.
20. Association of American Medical Colleges. https://www.aamc.org/download/68806/data/road-doctor.pdf. Accessed November 6, 2016.